The Average Person's Guide to POWER

by

Ike Smith

ISBN 978-0-615-44835-0

Table of Contents

Just Another Face

"You're just another person. At your funeral, besides your immediate family, the rest of the world will miss you as much as the passing wind. That's the way it is. If you're lucky, life won't be too hard on you." As a five year old I heard those fateful words from a relative.

At one point in my life I actually believed such words were true. As a nine-to-fiver, I recall during my morning commutes to work those words danced in my head, taunting me. They were like little needles lodged in my clothing near my lower back that pricked at my flesh with every forward motion I attempted to make in life. Frequently I'd scan the morning faces of other passengers during my train rides to work. Faces advertising the hopeless comfort of the daily grind in the land of khaki pants, staff uniforms and overpriced morning coffee wore blank stares that echo each day's obligations.

During every morning and evening rush hour, as everyone crammed into one train car attempting to somehow hold on to their individuality by enforcing personal space zones impossible to maintain during shoulder-to-shoulder, hip-to-hip train rides destined for our obligatory responsibilities, I'd think. You're just another person. Such words were like tiny rocks at the bottom of my feet, nestled into the fibers of my socks. That's the way it is.

Harboring those words often left me with a heavy feeling. An emotional tug that can only be described as a tormenting urge to act showed me no mercy. Drenching my face and posture at the start of every work week like a damp rug thrown on my reluctant shoulders. As I rode the morning train to a job that simply paid the bills yet cost me nearly every ounce of dignity to remain employed, I did not feel fulfilled. Yet, things could have been worse. At least I had a job. At least I was not homeless. At least I was not a total failure in life. If you're lucky, life won't be too hard on you.

In my head I heard a monotonous voice, sometimes my own or someone in my past that spoke to something in me which I scorned. This voice assaulted my psyche with words like: common, ordinary, standard and unspectacular. My relative's prediction for my life seemed to ring true. At your funeral, besides your immediate family the rest of the world will miss you as much as the passing wind.

Such undermining saboteurs the voices of reason can play on our minds and thinking. I hated such thoughts. What if I am just another person, soon to be dead and a distant memory to my loved ones? Could it be true that I am irrelevant to the rest of the planet? What if you are too?

As your hands cradle this book I ask, have you ever felt vulnerable to the possibility of being insignificant?

Usual, typical, mediocre- all terms that describe what it means to be average. Consider if any of those terms describe you in some way. Then answer this question: Are you an average person?

Chances are that you picked up this book because you feel that some part of you is as unspectacular as a random pebble under country road gravel. A strong possibility exists that you know the same persistent feeling I once knew after hearing that I was "just another person on the planet." It is also very likely you are tired of feeling so average that you occasionally ask yourself, "Is this really all I can be? Am I truly happy with this?"

Though some reasons may vary from one individual to the next, the term "average" applies to all of us in one way or many. Hence, the underlying motivation of everyone reading this book is the same: you do not want to be average in some area of your life anymore. More is what you want. But what does "more" mean for you? Also, how will "more" fulfill your life?

Frankly, you want your time on this planet to be more than just satisfying. At the very least, you crave another shot at something that defies your self-described mediocrity. Patience is a virtue but time waits for no one. Did your real life start or begin again yet? Be honest.

At 18, describe your life. At 30, what can you say for yourself? Is 40 the new 30 for you? At half a century, are any of us guaranteed another 50 years to take advantage of our earned wisdom?

Time flies whether you're having fun or not. So ponder the following. Your life now equals every thought, action and outcome connecting you to conditions affecting and influenced by your existence. So you have perfectly succeeded in getting where you are in life at this very moment. Should I sympathize or congratulate you? Only you know the answer.

No one picks up this book to remain the same. Presently, you want something. You may even need something. I do not profess to know what your "something" is. Still, consider the answer to the following question: how will you feel if you never get that "something" in this lifetime?

Chapter 1: The Mindset Scale

A good friend of mine rehabilitates rundown real estate properties. Her investment partner and I once went with her to view an old single family home she intended to purchase. When we entered the dilapidated property, obvious was the reason the selling price was dirt cheap. Molded hardwood floors, a disgustingly eroded bathroom rotten with mildew, busted windows and rusted piping just to name a few obvious challenges. But what I remember most was the den next to one of the three bedrooms on the second floor of the home. Inside the den, we saw a giant hole in the wall which was easily large enough to not only see into the next room but I'm certain I could have climbed through the hole into the next bedroom.

At sight of the damaged wall, my friend's investment partner immediately claimed in frustration, "That hole is gigantic. It's going to be hard to patch up, it's too big. This isn't looking good so far." My friend responded, "That hole is perfect. We can just knock down the entire wall and create an oversized master bedroom twice the size as the other two bedrooms on this floor!"

She was right. It's not what you see but how you see it. Often what appears to be an obstacle is merely a clue that an opportunity awaits. With the right perception in place to demonstrate a proactive mindset, my friend used an unattractive hole in the wall to envision a huge master bedroom area that eventually added needed value to an undervalued property. Take heed. No one obtains the Higher Power Mindset with viewpoints and behavior committed to mediocrity due to flawed or limited perceptions. Your perceptions, mindset and behavior reveal your own perceptual conditioning. In your own head is where your personal power is birthed. Great people see the world in unique ways.

Perceptual conditioning is an ongoing internal and external process. It is an intricate, co-dependent relationship between your mind and surrounding influences. As a whole, you represent both internal and external perceptual conditioning. Internally, you embody genetics, feelings, beliefs and convictions. External factors like people and circumstances play a part in molding your perceptions.

Simply put, at times your genetics, feelings, beliefs and convictions will determine how you perceive the world. Other times, the world will impact your genetics, feelings, beliefs and convictions to alter or enhance your perceptions. The balance you adopt between both internal and external determinants is demonstrated in your mindset.

With such complexity, how can you begin assessing your current mindset? If you conclude that your own feelings and beliefs solely represent your mindset, you ignore the influences of external factors like the environment. On the other hand, if you determine that your mindset is a direct result of external influences, you neglect the impact that your own beliefs and feelings have on your perceptions.

When speaking with clients, I always ask them, "Do you believe more in destiny or choice?" Such a question challenges my clients to assess how much power they grant external forces like people or circumstances versus their own thoughts, beliefs, convictions and perceptions within their control. In essence, whether you believe your path is predetermined, chosen or a combination of both- your mindset determines the actions you take. The choices you execute land you in good or bad places. If you are unhappy, unfulfilled or considering expanding your present life circumstances then examining and adjusting your mindset is the first step. This chapter invites you to explore your own Mindset Scale.

How do you see?
Picture a two-sided weight scale. In the center of the scale is an adjustable balance point which can be manipulated left or right. On the left side of the scale is the world: people, established societies, cultures and ways of living. On the right side of the two-sided scale is your mind: thoughts, beliefs, personal values and convictions. As you visualize both, which of the two weigh the most in your life?

Compare both sides of the scale. If the world weighs more, the left side of the scale will be lower while the right side is higher in the air. Those of you that envision the world as a heavier force on your scale are heavily influenced by your surroundings.

On the contrary, a heavier right side will show your mind lower on the scale while the world is raised higher. If you imagined your mind as the heavier factor on the scale, your own thoughts, beliefs, personal values and convictions greatly impact your perceptions.

Resting at the same height, both the right and left side will be at equal.   A balanced scale hints at a balanced outlook. How does your scale look?

In all fairness, the above example is oversimplified. The positioning of your mindset scale varies depending on one thing-the central, adjustable balance point of the scale. You can adjust the central point at any time giving more weight to the world or your own mind. It's your choice. The option is simply available. But recognizing, embracing and effectively handling such power is not simple.

When the world appears overwhelming or intimidating to such a degree that you feel controlled, helpless or defeated your mind wanders, high in the air dangling in the wind. Picture a bitter, pessimistic person that claims "things are how they are" and "there's no point in trying because the end is near." To such a person, the world is a big heavy place.

Yet when your mind becomes so dominant, controlling and closed, heaviness occurs and the world around you becomes smaller, lighter and insignificant when compared to your own thoughts, beliefs and convictions. Ever refused to change your mind? Ever objected to hearing an opposing opinion? If you've ever seen, experienced or demonstrated sexism, racism or classism you can understand what happens when the human mind is alienated or seemingly immune to outside or opposing influences. Small minds result and live in small worlds. Extreme are the examples here to make a very crucial point: without balance, your mindset can and will take you into frighteningly extreme places.

With an imbalanced mindset increased are the chances for you to create negative outcomes, whether exemplified as heartless and oppressive behavior or masked as noble, self-righteousness. When your mindset lacks a central presence of well-roundedness, extreme thoughts, beliefs, convictions and eventually actions erupt in ways that sometimes defy logic and all forms of morality. When this occurs, you have either forgotten or neglected to realize that you always have a choice in how you perceive things just as much as you can decide your own actions.

On a daily basis, you select perspectives. A rising sun signals a new day or another day closer to death. Your journey is a long road ahead or gained ground. Obstacles you face could be mountains blocking your path or signs that there is higher ground. Which perspectives dominate your reality? Your perceptual conditioning helps mold your mindset which guides your actions. Have your actions led to more failures or successes? If you do not like the answer to that question, or want to improve your response, know that your journey beyond mediocrity begins in your own mind.

Some people only see what they want to see. Other people just see what they need to see. Powerful people see what they need to see in order to see what they want to see. How do you see things?

You have a mindset. We all do. So distinct are the various outlooks in this world that we've come up with seemingly endless ways to label mental outlooks. Optimistic, pessimistic, realistic or idealistic- the list is extensive. No one person exhibits the same outlook in all situations. However, we all have a consistent mindset that we resort to in most situations. Perceptual conditioning and behavioral patterns can be found in all of us. How else do we begin to categorize or label people as optimists, pessimists or idealists?

Still, do not mistake your own perceptual conditioning as unchangeable. All habits are made over time and can be broken as well. You should first understand how such perceptual habits formed. The average person's guide to power lies in mastering his or her perceptions.

In daily life, all of us are guilty of sometimes perceiving things the wrong way. Unfairly judging others, situations and obstacles hinder our perspectives. Racism, sexism and all forms of discrimination are a few of the unfortunate results of skewed or misguided perceptions that negatively impact our societies, nothing good results.

Where is the source of such disruptions?

Blame the most important half of the Mindset Scale: your mental outlook. Though this world and your mindset have a cyclical relationship, it is your mindset that is most important to focus on now. You may want to alter realities surrounding your circumstances. But do not focus on the external part of the mindset scale yet. For now, your mental outlook is the central opportunity for change and focus because you have immediate access to your own frame of mind. In other words, let's focus on exploring the exactness of your mindset.

The Mental Triad
Your mind is comprised of a Mental Triad that includes your Natural, Inherited and Higher Self. All three parts coexist. Every perception formed and decision made is impacted by your Mental Triad. Outcomes which you experienced resulting from choices

you made can all be traced back to your Mental Triad to such a degree that your mindset at the time you made any choice can be unveiled. Whether you made your decision as your Natural, Inherited or Higher Self can be discovered.

You are born as your Natural Self.

You are handed your Inherited Self by others and the environment.

Your Higher Self is eventually achieved to govern your Natural and Inherited selves.

All three parts are essential and provide insight into your personal truths. But not all parts have equal power over you. At various times during your psychological and emotional growth, one part will have more influence than the other two, depending on your maturity and the circumstances. Also, two parts can dominate one on occasions. Your Natural, Inherited and Higher Self will not always exhibit a healthy, balanced Mental Triad. If you grasp and embrace how all three elements work individually and together to shape your mindset, better self-management results. To truly comprehend the next three chapters and obtain the Higher Power Mindset, you need to adopt the correct understanding of your own mental outlook by the end of this very essential chapter.

Your Natural Self

Do you remember your own birth? Is there any chance you can recall your very first steps as a child? Your first words, do you remember them? Forgotten experiences will be your response, no doubt.

I'd like you to obtain two things before reading any further. You will need a piece of paper and pen.

Next I want you to think back and try to remember your earliest memory. This memory may not be complete or even make sense to you now. Cohesiveness is not important. I just need you to remember as much about your earliest memory as possible: colors, locations, scents, sounds and feelings. Write down everything associated with your earliest memory that your mind can recall.

Secondly, I want you to find out how old you were at the time that your memory took place. The memory and your age are important pieces of information if you are to comprehend the sections ahead.

Assuming you have completed my requests, we can now begin to explore the first part of your Mental Triad: the Natural Self.

At birth, your Natural Self was similar to an unplanted seed. Despite your small size and vulnerability as a new life in this world, possessed by your Natural Self were all of your potential, genetic dispositions, personality traits and temperament like a seed awaiting fertilization. Though not fully matured, you were not only a bundle of joy but a huge life of new promise.

For the sake of understanding, I now want you to visualize your Natural Self as a multi-colored seed in red, yellow, blue and green. The red part of the seed represents your physical make-up. Yellow represents your personality traits. Blue signifies your brain. Green represents your unique, outstanding gift or ability. Undeveloped but existent, such a colorful seed holds so much power. If nurtured and cultivated properly, the seed will grow to its potential.

Now take notice of the age in which your first memory took place. For most of you, age two or three will be most common. Yet, I've known people who have an earliest memory dating back to even sooner than two or three years old. Regardless of the age you wrote down, what I want you to understand is that the age you recorded marks the transformation of your Natural Self into your Inherited Self, which we will explore shortly. For now, our focus is on your life before your earliest memory. It is at that time, before your earliest memory, that your Natural Self was most unaffected.

Born from two people, you naturally inherited genetics, physical and psychological dispositions from your birth parents. Picture the seed of your Natural Self again, in red, yellow, blue and green. The red part of the seed represents your physical make-up. Yellow represents your personality traits. Blue signifies your brain. Green represents your unique, outstanding gift or ability.

Much like any seed, where it is planted matters greatly. Soil condition, the weather, and other external factors affect the growth of any seed. Similarly, the cultivation of your Natural Self was affected by where your life began. If you've ever seen a tree slanted heavily in one direction or another, if you've ever seen a plant that somehow grows through concrete or around a hard object like a post or fence, you've witnessed the instinct of survival at work.

All forms of life begin with inherent potential and the earliest stages of growth are most crucial. When you see a tree or plant oddly growing in unique directions, the seed adjusted to its environment. If a tree needs more sun, it will seek more sun by growing in the direction where more sun can be acquired. A plant needs the sun to keep growing upward, so if needed it will grow around obstructions to get what it needs for survival. Likewise, when you were born into your external environment the seed of your Natural Self began to seek ways to grow and survive.

Make no mistake in assuming otherwise, survival is the primary goal of any new life during the earliest, most vulnerable phases of development. Though your Natural Self was filled with potential to do many things, the most necessary demands were met first. For example, as a newborn you could not immediately speak the same language as your parents but you could make sounds that indicated hunger, irritation, fear and other emotions you felt. If you lived in a noisy environment, you probably learned to scream faster or louder than another infant that was submerged in an extremely quiet environment. In other words, though external challenges existed even as a newborn you began to find ways to obtain what you needed from those you depended upon.

Like clockwork, your body began to anticipate when you'd be fed, bathed and coddled. Your parents and caretakers will attest to this, when you did not get fed on time or held in the arms of a loved one enough, your tears and cries shared your feelings! In survival mode, your Natural Self began mapping your environment, anticipating the best ways to get food, warmth, water and your diaper changed. Even if your Natural Self contained a special gift like extraordinary intelligence, superb athletic ability or the potential to have the steady hands of surgeon, in your earliest years, getting your next meal took precedence over anything else. The development of special gifts would have to wait.

Now let's get back to the discussion of your first memory. At the age your first memory took place, before then your memory was not reliable. In fact, you probably learned to do many things before one or two years old but kept forgetting how to execute anything consistently because your brain was not ready to store and recall information for longer than a week or so. In short, you had to learn how to remember things.

Through much repetition and exposure, eventually your brain was able to store your first memory. Now examine your first recollection. Chances are that your memory is something you were exposed to repeatedly or traumatically. An impression was made frequently or emphatically enough that your first memory resulted and this marked a turning point in your own mental development and maturity. Affected most was your Natural Self.

Unfortunately, because your Natural Self was so vulnerable to your external environment and you were not able to fully articulate your own thoughts, feelings and inclinations, the chances of maximizing all aspects of your Natural Self decreased. Utilizing your new abilities to remember, talk, walk and cultivate your Inherited Self was necessary. Even if you embodied the potential to be the next technical guru, world leader or trend setting inventor, mastering how to walk, talk and recognize your given name was of prime importance.

In all fairness to parents, no child comes into the world with a sign which indicates his or her full potential. Just think if newborns came with labels that revealed their potential futures: Future Curer of Cancer, Future Discoverer of How to Live on Mars or Future World Leader that Will Ensure Peace. I think if we all were born with such signs, our parents would have done their best to make sure we reached our destinations. Since that is not the case, most parents do what they can do to love, protect and nurture their children in hopes of raising happy, fulfilled individuals that reach whatever potential is possible. Though parental and environmental influences play impactful roles in whether or not you reach your potential or not, ultimately the biggest influence rests with you.

I've asked you to explore your earliest memory and identify at what age that memory took place for one reason: you may have lost or neglected a part of your Natural Self which could be a key to fulfilling your fullest potential and obtaining the Higher Power Mindset.

What if you left a part of your Natural Self underdeveloped? Perhaps part of the seed that is your Natural Self was never required for survival during your first years. Parts of the brain go unused when not needed or utilized. Like the muscles on your body that are underutilized, naturally such muscles are weaker than other muscles you use daily. Such disparity in strength can also translate to the brain as well. As your brain utilizes areas crucial to body movement, motions unfamiliar or not needed for your survival get neglected. Which means that if you attempt to execute a back flip despite the fact that you have never done so before, you will fail because not only is your body not conditioned to complete the back flip, your brain is not either.

If you've ever had trouble remembering how to do something that you previously were able to do, like sew or throw a ball, you understand how it feels to be "rusty" at doing something. The brain is no different than your leg muscles, biceps or abdominals, if you don't use it, you can lose it- or at least have a very hard time developing what you neglected. Your Natural Self is still inside you. Some part of it is still in its infant or toddler stages.

Picture the seed of your Natural Self again, in red, yellow, blue and green.

The red part of the seed represents your physical make-up- maybe you've grown into a healthy, fit adult or morphed into a body full of health problems.

Yellow represents your personality traits- perhaps you've developed sound confidence and a positive demeanor or you could be full of psychologically crippling insecurities and an unpleasant demeanor.

Blue signifies your brain- conceivably you could be a brilliant intellectual or an underachieving high school dropout.

Green represents your unique, outstanding gift or ability- do you know what it is?

The point is that right now, you want something more than what you have in your life. A complete and honest introspective look is required. You need to fix, improve weaknesses or discover new gifts that you possibly neglected at a defining time in your life. I believe you already have what it takes inside of you. You just have to find it again.

Urges, impulses, instincts and occasionally behavioral outbursts all unveil parts of you. Something keeps telling you to do something, be something, feel something and live more. That something is your forgotten Natural Self, hidden underneath what took place at the age when you recalled your first memory.

We are all born with natural tendencies, uninterrupted characteristics. Some of us are naturally inclined to be passive, aggressive, inquisitive, outgoing or even shy. As a child, your natural inclinations were purest. Before life experiences demanded maturation, childlike impulses ruled your thoughts, feelings and actions.

Think of watching two different 2 or 3 year old children on a playground during summer. One may approach the play area with reckless abandon, while the other timidly explores the playground as if inspecting for hidden traps. To adults the world is perceived through experienced eyes. But to growing kids with inexperienced outlooks, surroundings embody an entirely new world of mystery.

Visualize yourself in a foreign land minus knowledge of the language or customs and you will get a sense of what young children face. Under such conditions natural inclinations of any human being are purely instinctive impulses aimed at gaining some measure of understanding through experience and eventually control. Free of cultural biases, social norms and demands, the Natural Self represents the sort of naivety and truthfulness only found before life experiences and others shaped us.

Once I was jogging through a neighborhood. On the front lawn of a beautiful home were four young boys that looked to be about 2 or 3 years old. One African-American, White, Hispanic and Oriental- they were playing with a tiny football. Playful, joyous and carefree, the young boys seemed completely unaware that possibly twenty years from that day they will be aware of racism and violence.

Oblivious to the concept of discrimination, politics, money and war, the four young lads did what came natural to them. They enjoyed life free of tainted perceptions and limitations on what it means to be a human being. In their minds, they were not members of a specific ethnic group or economic class but four kids that enjoyed tossing around the pigskin on a warm afternoon.

Though romanticized and idealistic, can you think back to your innocence? Before you knew what getting top grades in class meant, previous to realizing that your family was rich or poor compared to others, you could care less about what your credit score and job title represented. Those things did not matter to your Natural Self.

Family responsibilities, employment obligations, utility bills, taxes, rent or mortgages had no meaning in the world of your early youth. What made you happy brought a smile to your face. A frown or free flowing tears signaled your good time was interrupted or ended. You felt what you felt without second thoughts about political correctness or moral implications. Life was simple.

Perhaps your eyes gravitated to architecture.

Maybe your voice sang words you did not understand but your heart loved to sing. Running into the wind was probably your favorite hobby. Taking a bath to you was like swimming for the country's Olympic team.

In short, your passions and gifts flowed freely at this stage.

Chocolate chips cookies for breakfast seemed normal to you then. Bowls and bowls of your favorite cereal for dinner suited you just fine and vegetables ruined every meal. Yes, you would wear the same pair of your favorite purple pants, red gym shoes and a faded orange t-shirt everyday if your mother did not impede on your budding sense of fashion. While adults perceived you as a self-centered, egotistical child that just didn't know any better. Your Natural Self was at play. Free and uninhibited by self-conscious impulses, expression was not only easy but necessary.

Many underestimate just how sincere we all were in the beginning or our lives. We often chalk up such childish memories as "kid stuff." We even forget.

Once I was at my grandmother's home with my mother viewing an old photo album. In almost every picture I was laughing and playing but seemed to never have a shirt on! I asked my mother, "Why in the world am I shirtless in every picture?" She said, "Whenever you were having a good time with your cousins, you'd just take your shirt off and run around freely playing tag. You despised t-shirts."

I was a little embarrassed. In each picture I was a scrawny little two year old kid. Furthermore, I had no memory whatsoever of taking any of the photos or preferring to be shirtless all the time. To my own amazement, I could not account for some of the most joyous times in my childhood.

As you age, layers of social norms merge over your impulses, thoughts and most instinctive behaviors. We mature. Slowly but surely, the next state of mind begins to overlap your Natural Self, sometimes at the expense of even your special gifts and abilities.

Your Inherited Self
Recall your earliest memory and when the experience took place. At that age, you started accepting your Inherited Self. With the improved ability to recall and store memories your capacity to learn from your experiences increased. Forming associations and understanding the context in which those associations belonged became a part of your elevated state of consciousness as your Inherited Self formed.

What is your name? Someone assigned it to you at birth and after hearing it repeatedly from those around you, you began to recognize the sound of it. Eventually you grasped that whenever you heard that name it was somehow associated with you so you responded. Placing your name into the context of your own identity resulted.

What nationality are you? Our society branded your heritage. Someone informed you of your cultural identity: Irish, Italian, Russian, African or some other nationality. Again, just as you did with your own name, you formed associations and contexts around your own nationality. More of your identity was established.

What is your gender? Believe it or not, you were not always aware that you are either male or female. Someone informed you of your sex at some point in time. Even the style of your name derives from cultural and gender influences.

The most basic yet absolutely essential of identifications assigned to you came from others around you so that you could form associations and create contexts which would ground your own identity. Your external environment helped shape you. Yet how you process and utilize your own internal truths and information which relate to your environment is what cultivates and essentially define your Inherited Self.

In fact, until your Higher Self is achieved, most of your life you will process and respond to external influences in the state of mind established by your Inherited Self. Meaning that at this very moment it is highly plausible that up until this point in your life, the concept of having a Higher Self is new to you as you've been operating in life as your Inherited Self for so long.

Your family and environment helped transform your Natural Self into your Inherited Self. I refer to this process as perceptual conditioning, which either upholds or overwhelms your natural inclinations if those impulses align or conflict with socially acceptable behavior. For example, while a toddler when your Natural Self decided it was time to go "potty" you just did it, wherever and whenever the inclination arose. Consequences, opinions of others and the smell of your own waste were none of your concerns. Through "potty training" from those taking care of you, your Natural Self learned when and how to relieve yourself in a more socially acceptable manner- in a bathroom instead of a diaper. Luckily for all involved in your "potty training," your Inherited Self accepted the socialization to avoid the stresses that acting as your Natural Self would bring!

Educated in your local school systems, you learned to read, write and count. Socially groomed by your family, loved ones and communities, you inherited your first lifestyle. Thanks to a specific community of social norms your socio-economic background formed.

A child growing up in New York will differ significantly in speech and behavior from a child maturing in Boise, Idaho. A woman born and raised in China will differ from a woman born and raised in the United States. A young man accustomed to life on a farm may find urban environments extremely different than his normal dwellings.

None of us can choose our parents or where our life begins on this planet. We simply adapt to our environment with our own Natural Selves until our Inherited Selves learn how to cope with our surrounding truths.

Like a teacher instructs a student in school, the perceptions of others reached you. As you mastered your language, adopted acceptable social nuances, unknowingly embraced an accent that reflects your region, the personality of your Inherited Self found life.

Some of us were told by parents and authority figures to go to school, get good grades so we can go to college, study a career, graduate from a higher learning institution and secure a job that will help us establish financial security. Some of us were told to hustle, do whatever it takes to get what you want and need because the ends justify the means. Many of us were sold on the idea that what comes around goes around, so do good and goodness will find us. Some of us were convinced that life is about the survival of the fittest not the nicest. Every one of us at one point or another accepted the ideas and beliefs of others to establish the foundation of our mental outlook. Fully embracing our Inherited Self, we marched through life expecting results explained or experienced by others before us.

I can recall so many times sitting in a college classroom as an undergraduate. Listening to instructors recite theories and research findings of other great thinkers. Watching ambitious students display their knowledge and appreciation of other great minds before them by reading books and imitating their favorite role models, how impressionable we all are I thought.

While studying and understanding forms of greatness before us is indeed valuable, I knew in my heart that life as a chronic student of others was not the way to greatness. Eventually we all have to step beyond theories, research, books and our socioeconomic backgrounds. In time we all are challenged to either be well informed disciples of those that crafted new paths and made new discoveries. Or we can endure the trying stages of success and failure on our own, as other great minds did, to form our own new paths and validate our own opinions and outlooks on life. While all of us may draw similar ideas and conclusions, by way of personal experience we can at least say that the findings and outcomes are truly our own.

You are at a crossroads if you hold this book in your hands. As your Inherited Self you have successfully secured your current place in life. Look around. Take in the results. Decide how you feel about what your present life represents about you and your past choices. Ironically, had you been born in another country, introduced to another language, culture, spiritual and even political ideology as a child- you would not be who you are presently. Imagine if you grew up in another neighborhood, city, state, region or country.

Sadly, some of you will have trouble fathoming such possibilities. But the existence of chance plays a role in all of our lives. Though I am writing this book in English because I was born in Chicago, Illinois (USA), I could have easily been born on the island of Borneo located southwest of the Philippines. Then I'd possibly be speaking Oma Lung or Uma Kulit, which are two Kenyah languages of Borneo. Such undeniable possibilities exist. Your Inherited Self was implanted in you because you happened to be born at a specific time and place. Do not be fooled into believing that your way of living and viewpoint is the absolute and complete truth for you. There is also more to learn and experience. Of course, that is why you picked up this book.

A certain impulse, urge or instinct exists in you now. The reason you are at a crossroads presently is because internal conflict exists in you. For some this conflict may be intense or even dark, for others it may be revelations, light or elated sensations seeking even more life fulfillment. Either way, I can explain what you are feeling and why.

Natural Self versus Inherited Self
Eventually conflict emerged between your Natural and Inherited Self. Remember earlier in the chapter when I stated that because your Natural Self was so vulnerable to your external environment and you were not able to fully articulate your own thoughts, feelings and inclinations, the chances of maximizing every aspect of your Natural Self decreased. I've asked you to explore your earliest memory and identify at what age that memory took place for one reason: you may have neglected a part of your Natural Self which could be a key to fulfilling your fullest potential and obtaining the Higher Power Mindset.

Part of the seed that is your Natural Self was never required for survival during your first years so it was pushed aside. But your Natural Self is still inside you. Some part of it lives awaiting your attention.

Here's why I believe you already have what it takes inside of you to obtain the Higher Power Mindset. Urges, impulses, instincts and occasionally behavioral outbursts all describe you at times. Something keeps telling you to do something, be something, feel something and live more. That something is your forgotten Natural Self, hidden underneath what took place at the age when you recalled your first memory.

You have reached a point where your Natural Self felt smothered. Missing was something from your present life. Sleepless nights, reoccurring thoughts, nagging impulses that lack direction are all symptoms. Maybe you've endured repeated outcomes that have finally convinced you of your own inability to break cycles of behavior in your life.

Admittedly, I went through a phase in my life where every two years I had to find a new job, even when I experienced exceptional success in my positions. I would always start off doing outstanding work for a superior that took great joy in my results, then I'd get promoted one level up within a year or less, perform outstanding for another year and hit a glass ceiling at the end of year two, despite stellar performance reviews and achievements. I heard all sorts of reasons from organizational higher-ups as to why my advancement would stop: budget restraints, reorganization initiatives, racism and even that I was too good to promote because my services were so desperately needed where I was already. I learned that none of the reasons provided were sufficient.

The fact is: I'd reached my crossroads. My Inherited Self had outgrown mediocre surroundings and results. My work was exceptional but my rewards were limited by the organizations and their budgets, competitive hierarchies, office politics and the fact that I owned nothing and was simply a small part of the organizational puzzle. My Inherited Self thought, "Work harder, work longer, make the right friends and protect your position so that you can have job security."

But my Natural Self voiced in my head, "You'll never get paid what you deserve unless you take more risks, own your work and reap all the benefits of your rewards. You're limited when you work for others. You can't use all of your skills because your assigned job description is the glass ceiling. You could do extra work but you'll just get a pat on the back and still the same salary. You are a creator, so create unlimited possibilities for yourself!"

I'm willing to bet you have an internal conflict of some sort as well. At different points in time, you've felt such feelings before. Perhaps you began disagreeing with your parents on issues, rebelling against authority figures and even defying rules imposed on your life that previously your Inherited Self accepted without question. Can you remember the first time you ever asked an authority figure, "Why can't I do what I want to do?"

I can recall when I was five years old I defied my mother. We lived on Chicago's West Side in a small apartment complex on a street named Kostner. Always busy with traffic, I was used to hearing cars zoom past at all times of day and night because the street was an exit for the local highway.

As a kindergartener, I attended a nearby school located just down the street from my apartment complex. Every day after school I walked home with my classmate Al and his older brother Henry, a fifth grader.

One day after school, Henry did not arrive to walk home with us. So Al and I walked alone. However, Al lived across the street from me on the busy avenue of Kostner and did not know how to cross the street.

I had never crossed the street alone either. Plus, my mother reminded me repeatedly not to attempt to cross Kostner without her. Once Al and I reached my apartment I was at odds with my mother's command versus helping my friend Al get home. Al asked, "Can you walk me across the street?"

I was afraid. My mother's warnings screamed through my mind. But my Natural Self was excited at the new challenge. Anticipating the freedom of marching out into the street and conquering the forbidden territory fueled my natural inclination toward new challenges. Inside me emerged a gravitational pull aimed at the prospect of proving to my mother I was bold and smart enough to cross the busy street alone.

But my Inherited Self would not shut up!

My mother's words left foot prints on my brain as my Inherited Self began to recite my mom's words in the exact tone, pace and voice inflections as the actual moments I'd experienced face to face with her. It seemed like she was standing next to me on the curb as I stood there trying to act confident for my friend Al. "Son, don't you dare cross that street. You're too young, too small and the cars can't see you. Wait for an adult." Still I contemplated.

No, I'd never crossed the street alone before. Yes, I'd always obeyed my mother. But on that day, my Natural Self took my Inherited Self by the throat and screamed, "Why can't I cross the street? What's the big deal? Sooner or later, one day I'm going to walk across this street. So I may as well do it now. Be quiet and let me concentrate!"

I looked at Al and said, "Don't worry Al, I'll get you across."

I took Al's hand, peered out into the street searching in both directions for oncoming vehicles. The coast was clear. I tugged Al's hand and we marched across the street with such ease that I remember thinking, "I can't believe I ever feared this street."

Once across, Al smiled at me as if I was his new hero. He ran off to his apartment. Full of pride, I watched Al scurry into his place. My Natural Self proceeded to address my Inherited Self, "How could you ever have doubted me? You are such a chicken. From now on, I'm in charge here so don't forget it."

Still glowing from my conquest, my Natural Self and I proceeded to step back into the street to head home and brag to my mother how we crossed the street without her.

BLAM! The only problem was that I was now flying in the air toward a light post that was aimed at my right shoulder. I landed against the pole, bounced off to get slung back into the street then landed on my back. Looking up, I could see the silver rear bumper of a green vehicle stopped a few feet in front of me. I'd been struck by a speeding car.

Dazed like I'd been sucker punched by a professional heavyweight boxer, I wobbled to my feet stunned and confused. Without much coordination, I remember walking toward my apartment. All traffic stopped as I slowly staggered in the middle of the street. Car horns were blowing. My head buzzed with ringing sounds. People had exited their vehicles and were watching me wobble across the street, stumble back onto the sidewalk in front of my apartment complex and crawl up the stairs into my hallway. Falling up the stairs repeatedly, I made it to the door of my apartment and managed to even unlock the door with my key.

Once inside, I'd regained my focus enough to grab a donut off the table, head to my living room sofa, sit down and stare blankly at the television while munching on my donut. I did not say a word to my mother who was in her room. "See, I told you not to cross that street," my Inherited Self gloated.

Minutes later, there was a knock at the door. My mother answered. Two men proceeded to tell her that they'd hit me with their green car moments earlier. They came to see if I was ok. I was, unmarked and unbroken physically. But my Natural Self had a bruised ego, while my Inherited Self basked in the righteous light of correctness. My mother was shocked and could only stare at me in complete disbelief as I sat on the sofa wondering, "I hope she doesn't spank me, I think I've been hit one too many times already today." She didn't. But she did take me to the emergency room to ensure I was not injured. Amazingly, I was unharmed. She grounded me shortly afterwards.

As you can see, internal conflict between your Natural and Inherited Selves breed confusion and even bad decisions. Much like your own internal urges from your Natural Self which now challenge the conventional status of your Inherited Self, my urge to cross the street challenged the inherited rules handed to me by my mother. Unfortunately, my natural inclination to be adventurous and brave was misplaced at the time I attempted to cross the busy street as a 5 year old. Obviously, my Inherited Self lost that battle with my Natural Self.

In your own life knowing exactly what your Natural Self needs to be properly cultivated and utilized will be difficult initially. Especially when your more natural impulses have been pushed aside by the rationale of your Inherited Self for so long, mistakes will happen.

Whether you are a business executive with a deep longing to make a living as a painter or a bus driver that really wants to be a professional athlete, sometimes what your Inherited Self has helped you achieve, your Natural Self will want to go against. If this conflict is not resolved well, you can end up enduring more struggles than needed.

Your Natural Self may contain your passions, interests and some daring impulses. But your Inherited Self abides by social rules and perceptions which help you function in your current environment. Though your Inherited Self seems to stifle you in some ways and should be challenged when your outlook needs to be changed or expanded, its presence is necessary to compete with the sometimes reckless and irresponsible aspects of your Natural Self.

At times, your Inherited Self will win the battle and reduce the ramblings of your Natural Self into immature urges to be swept away for more grown-up choices. Other times, your Natural Self can overpower your inherited impulses and you'll take more risks. Sometimes this is good, especially when a situation demands your most natural instincts.

Overall, too much friction between the two states of mind is a sign that something is missing, an imbalance exists. Sometimes the transition from your Natural to Inherited Self is rocky. Stagnation can even occur as one of the parts resists and wins for a spell. Relapses back to immature ways when challenges erupt are not unlikely when the Natural Self defeats your inherited nature. Holding in raw emotions or creating clever tactics of denial can happen also as your Inherited Self tames your Natural Self. A harmonious balance is difficult to obtain.

At this tumultuous stage many people stop growing and never get to cultivate their Higher Self. Dangerously common is this outcome, which is why a book like this exists. Believe it or not, some of us are stuck, trapped at a certain stage of maturity despite our actual age. A 30 year old person can still have the mind of a 19 year old, if their Natural and Inherited Self maintains a longstanding feud.

Don't get me wrong, there is nothing wrong with having parts of your Inherited Self in your current character, especially if such a foundation has brought you good results. However, if you are finding that outcomes in your life too often are not what you want, there is a problem. The friction has to end. How can you know if the conflict between your Natural and Inherited Selves has reached a feverish level? Here are four common signs:

- Habitual Behavior: If it seems that no matter what you say or do, you keep repeating the same behaviors only to experience familiar outcomes.
- Confusion: Frequently in a state of complacency and insecurity, you habitually second-guess or regret your choices.
- Unsatisfied: You have achieved what you wanted, possess things you desired and seem to have life figured out. But you are unfulfilled and still long for something more but have no idea what to do about your emptiness.
- Resentfulness: Anger, bitterness, vindictiveness and disgust are a part of your daily emotions. Whether from old memories or present consequences from negative outcomes, no matter how hard you try you just can't leave the past out of your present or future.

So how does one outgrow the battle between the Natural and Inherited Self?

You must achieve your Higher Self. Governing both your Natural and Inherited Self is the job of your Higher Self. So an important question remains.

What is the first step to embodying your Higher Self? Back to the inherent right that all of us forget too frequently during life's challenges is now your focus. The answer begins with embracing the power of choice.

Choice

A very rich older man in his 60s took five thousand dollars out of his bank account. He placed the cash into a sealed white envelope and exited the bank. He set out to conduct an unusual test.

Upon seeing a tall, burly man in his 30s walking down the street, the rich man approached the husky stranger and stepped directly on the man's foot. The strong, stocky fellow winced in pain and then pushed the rich man to the ground and screamed, "Watch where you are going stupid!"

The rich man stood to his feet and walked onward. Next he saw a pretty woman walking toward him. She looked to be in her early 20s. The rich man walked up to her and stepped on her foot. The woman looked at the rich man, stepped on his feet then ran away.

The rich man walked onward once again. He saw an older gentleman in his 50s walking with a cane. The rich man approached him and knocked the cane out of the older gentleman's hand. The older man looked at the rich man and burst into laughter, offered his hand and shook hands with the rich man. Astounded and impressed, the rich man reached into his pocket and handed the older gentleman the white envelope filled with five thousand dollars in cash!

The older gentleman opened the white envelope, saw the money, smiled and started to cry. The rich man was now even more intrigued and asked, "Why are you crying? I just gave you five thousand dollars."

The old man stopped crying, smiled and then shouted, "I'm crying for the same reason you gave me this money: because I can!"

Did you know that the difference between an occurrence in your life and your response to that event is the key to interpreting if you have transcended the conflict between your Natural and Inherited Self? Please take a special note of the following sentence. When something happens to you, you have complete control over how you respond. What most people do not embrace is their inherent power of choice.

We forget that instead of losing our tempers, focus, motivation or sense of hope that we can decide how our mental outlook and emotions are affected. Such a truth appears easier said than done because happenings in our lives do not always warn or prep us before intruding on our existence. Sometimes we just react due to habitual conditioning. Other times we are overwhelmed and feel as if we have no choice but to succumb to the first impulse that triggers our emotions and behaviors. As fantastical as this reads: you always have a choice in how you respond.

Too simple, too good to be true and not realistic is how you may think such self control is. No way can anyone always decide their response to life events. What about raw emotions? What about instincts? Sometimes we just cannot help ourselves, no one is perfect. Yet none of us have to be perfect to always remind ourselves we have options when reacting.

When the rich man stepped on the husky man's foot, the strong stranger decided to push the rich man to the ground. The woman opted to respond with revenge and then fear as she ran from the rich man. Yet the old man decided to respond to the rich man's peculiar test with laughter and tears. Each of the three people possessed the power of choice. They each picked how they reacted to the rich man.

Similarly, you too can choose how you respond to losing a job, gaining new opportunities and managing your daily challenges. Unfortunately, some of us fear all the multiple paths before us. Believe it or not, we do not always want options. Some people just want to be told what to do, how to react and what to do next. We can even fear or despise having too many choices.

"I don't know what happened, but I just reacted." "It's like I was not myself when I did it." "I couldn't help myself." "I couldn't keep it together, it was just too much." So easy is the decision to avoid responsibility. Very simple is the explanation for choices ruled by impulsiveness. Hard is the way to enlightened decision-making. What a powerful responsibility you wield when you own your reactions.

You can stubbornly remain enslaved to bad habits, wallow in confusion and remain unsatisfied and even resentful. But the results of your actions will echo the lack of harmony between your Natural and Inherited Self. So do not expect advantageous outcomes.

Or your power of choice can be a stabilizing force within your mental outlook. Accepting full responsibility for your reactions, feelings and thoughts will heighten your chances of self-regulating your own behavior. Self management means that you know what affects your thoughts and emotions well enough to begin consciously ensuring that intense emotions do not overwhelm your decision-making ability. We all have emotional triggers, events or scenarios that commonly engage our deepest thoughts and emotions. Situations that depress, discourage or even excite us can also trigger familiar internal reactions. Like pressing a piano key to hear a specific musical note or pulling the strings of a puppet to create movements, our emotions are connected to all sorts of external happenings. In your own life, think of events that always seem to excite or even overwhelm you.

A reckless driver can ignite your road rage, a song could bring you to tears or a statement from a stranger, coworker or loved one that misjudges your character could make you angry. As you live, you begin to notice that certain life events you encounter will cross your path more frequently than others. Almost as if your life keeps revisiting the same situations which feature new people playing old parts, cyclical behavior originates from conditioned emotional responses- internal reactions that create predictable behavioral patterns.

Reprogramming or altering your own emotional conditioning takes more than awareness of your internal triggers. Self-regulation will help you slow down your conditioned impulsive reactions. Still, making more powerful, effective choices requires you to graduate into the third part of your Mental Triad.

Your Higher Self
What would your most accomplished self look like?

Imagine the most ideal version of yourself and what you're visualizing is your Higher Self. Embodied are all of your truest beliefs, convictions and values. Contained in your Higher Self is all of your greatest knowledge and wisdom beyond belief. Represented in your Higher Self is honesty and profound insight. Connected to your Higher Self is power which acts as the final voice in your head, the most trustworthy and reliable influence over your life. This book aims to guide you into securing and maintaining your Higher Self.

I was once told by a misguided teacher that, "No one can fix themselves because the problem originated with them in the first place. Someone else has to fix it for them."

I do not subscribe to such limitations, especially with my Higher Self as my guide. While I do believe that obtaining counseling and therapy can be beneficial for those needing guidance. I do not believe in creating dependency in those needing help. The goal of any responsible life changer is to empower those influenced to eventually treat, maintain and solidify themselves. While an objective helping hand is sometimes needed, such a strategy should not be the long term stabilizing force.

You can help yourself. You can solve your own problems. You can ask yourself tough questions and be honest with yourself. You can even nurture yourself to outgrow your Inherited Self into your Higher Self. Though your process of re-shaping your inherited perceptions may be difficult, the journey is not impossible to complete.

Especially since you now accept the power of choice into your mental outlook. At this stage I challenge you to not only comprehend your Natural and Inherited Self. In addition, I want you to ask yourself three questions:

Do you believe that you determine the outcomes in your life?

Do you believe that external factors determine the outcomes in your life?

Or do you believe that both you and external factors determine the outcomes in your life?

Take some time to answer each question honestly. Your responses unveil your mental outlook. For the remainder of this book, the type of mental outlook you adopt will determine how you interpret the upcoming chapters. Choose wisely.

If you believe that you determine the outcomes in your life, you assume that you have a high level of control over your own life. Unfortunately, this sort of mindset is imbalanced. Most of the information ahead will help you, but the final chapter will discourage your notion of how much control you actually have in your own life. I urge you to be open to new ideas that will expand your already strong mental outlook.

If you believe that external factors determine the outcomes of your life then you believe in destiny, fate and that your path has already been decided by forces other than you. Sadly, most of the information in the next three chapters will defy many of your beliefs and cause you some discomfort. Still, I invite you to endure a life altering experience by way of this book to add more power to your great respect for external influences.

However, if you believe that both you and external factors determine the outcomes in life, I commend you. The mental outlook you embrace is perfect for this book. You are on your way to maximizing your Mental Triad by developing your Higher Self.

I must warn you though. The upcoming expedition is not easy. By now, you know and understand your own Natural and Inherited Self. What you need at this point is to develop the proper foundation of principles for your Higher Self to emerge in order to rule your Natural and Inherited Self.

The next three chapters will help. Three Superior Truths exposed ahead are universal principles crucial to growth. Only then can you embody the Higher Power Mindset.

Chapter 2: Change is Inevitable

"If it ain't broken, don't fix it." "Don't try and reinvent the wheel." "The more things change, the more things stay the same."

We've all heard those phrases at some point in our lives. Most of the time, such talk makes perfect sense. Especially if consistency is our goal and playing it safe appears to be the best option. Your Inherited Self surely appreciates the goal of consistency.

Why shake things up? Don't we have a responsibility and sometimes an obligation to just do the right thing and follow the norm? Supposedly, what works for most is best.

When ways of thought or action prove to consistently result in the "right" outcomes for people then the right thing to do often becomes the only thing to do. Fitting in with the norm is not shunned. It is encouraged.

Walk down the street and you'll notice the quiet but consistent social norms among us that make fitting in naturally appealing. For instance, consider the nonverbal action of eye contact. People usually avoid prolonged eye contact with strangers. Starring at a stranger for more than a second is often interpreted as rude, intrusive, or overtly flirtatious and in some cases a sign of aggression. We minimize the chances of offending or inviting a stranger into our personal space by remaining impersonal with our stares and glances. We follow the norm to demonstrate politeness and protect our own privacy.

On the other hand, exceptions exist even within social norms. Though a huge majority of people may agree that excessive eye contact is bothersome, another segment of people may welcome the deviation from that norm. Ever visited a small rural town? Compared to urban life, rural areas are sometimes more accepting of strangers. Eye contact is not always interpreted as intrusive but a sign of communicating friendliness. To some, a person that avoids eye contact has something to hide or cannot be trusted.

Though rare in some places, in other areas good eye contact with a stranger and a pleasant greeting is the norm. Anything other than a polite hello is viewed as rude or pretentious. Even though established normalcy often thrives among the masses, subsets of norms can still exist among us all.

But heed the following. When norms or traditions begin to represent morality, beware. Norms that morph into glorified traditions among people frequently begin to represent the actual moral codes of the group endorsing the popular benchmark. At that point, those that defy or differ are perceived as immoral, rebellious or wrong.

People can sometimes allow tradition or social norms to hinder independent thoughts, actions and even creativity. Your Natural Self when challenged by norms or traditions may ask, "Why not change?" Your Inherited Self will instinctively respond, "That's just how things are always done. Just do it."

Be mindful. Mediocrity is based on consistency. How many people do you know that are consistently good at not standing out? Recall individuals you witnessed go the extra mile just to fit in. The happy middle ground is home to many.

I do not mean to state that consistency is bad. What I want you to grasp is very simple. Eventually norms must be defied and consistency will not be enough for greatness. At times, the uncomfortable reality is that mediocrity will not be enough for you to feel challenged, fulfilled and successful.

Obtaining this book means that just getting by is just plain out of the question for you now. When the moment overwhelms you to do more, prove more and acquire more, give in. The title of this book is not, "How to Do Everything the Usual Way and Quietly Die as Another Anonymous Person that Did Everyone Else a Favor by Perfectly Fitting In."

Supporters of norms say, "If it ain't broke, don't fix it." In fact, quite the opposite is true. The premise of The First Universal Truth and basis of the Higher Power Mindset is: "It's never fixed so keep breaking it."

The First Universal Truth

The First Universal Truth is: change is ongoing and inevitable. Your power lies greatly in this fact. Change is a predetermined reality. Meaning, whether you like it or not, change occurs.

Nothing in life is ever complete. Incompleteness equates to vulnerability. Influence can be exerted on anything that is vulnerable in some way. Can you think of anything in life that does not change?

Just as the world around you keeps rotating, your life is just as dynamic. In essence, you are always a work in progress.

To many, the mere suggestion that change is inevitable echoes rebellion. Change signals something must be wrong. The comfort zone so often sought and supported by your Inherited Self is not satisfactory and the work is never finished once you embrace the true core of change. Old ways are not good anymore, traditions are threatened.

As you now accept The First Universal Truth of Change, circumstances conducive and resistant to change only mean that incompleteness exists. Things need to happen. Voids are present. Incompleteness allows room for you to take advantage and fill voids.

Know how to spot opportunities under any circumstances, good and bad. Remember to always search for, locate and exercise your power strands. Consider power strands like ropes of influence dangling from an endless sky. Much like grasping a rope to climb up a wall, power strands are what you find and pull. They represent access to influence, the very essence of power.

At all times you should ask yourself, "Where are the opportunities? What is within my grasp? What can I maximize to improve my situation now?"

Power strands dwell within the eternal process of change due to the incompleteness of the present. If you've ever witnessed change occur, whether new political movements, philosophies or even new management take over your department, change is not always welcomed. So I need you to completely comprehend just what I mean by the term "change." When you do, you'll know why change is so dynamic and feared, but an absolute blessing for the average person.

Change is eternal. Unfortunately, opportunity within change is only as dynamic as your frame of mind. Your Natural Self will be curiously excited. Your Inherited Self might be cautious or skeptical. How you mentally frame your surroundings and circumstances is crucial. See your surroundings with a power mindset and you will do more than see the world for what it could be, but what it is: yours.

Picture this world like a grid of moving dots. Chaotic dots moving forward, backward, vertical, horizontal, diagonal, cyclical and random directions unexpectedly. At times the dots intersect or get redirected by other dots. Sometimes dots even join together to form new dots. Each dot possesses its own origin, past, present and possible destinations. In this imaginary world of dots, nothing is ever motionless.

Similarly, our world is often viewed as chaotic and even unpredictable. How you frame what you see and experience in your mind determines your thoughts, beliefs, attitude and your behavior. It is best that you perceive as much truth as possible. The truth strengthens your foundation for planning and action.

In reality, our world is a collection of moving processes of history with endless possible outcomes. So each reality represents the past while simultaneously revealing the present with the potential for a dynamic future. Every person you meet and situation encountered is an incomplete and evolving, living truth. All situations, circumstances and outcomes can be categorized as one, some or all of the following: people-driven, natural processes and supernatural occurrences.

People-driven situations are created by the decisions and actions of human beings. Consider politics, education, technology or sports. Human input and participation are required.

Natural processes involve the laws of our physical universe. Rainfall, comets, gravity or earthquakes come to mind. Nature sustains our lives.

Supernatural truths represent the end of mankind's scientific knowledge and the beginning of something beyond the limits of our most sincere, complex thoughts, words and actions. We will explore this more in the final chapter.

Recognizing what type of change is taking place or possible in every situation heightens your awareness. The key to effective decision making is to accept the changing environment and embody some form of transitional truth. Do not underestimate the inevitability of change.

Even when we stop moving, everything else continues onward. Visualize standing in a busy airport terminal during holiday season. Picture yourself standing motionless in the middle of a busy highway during morning rush hour. How many people will you rub shoulders with or bump into at that busy airport terminal? How many enraged drivers will honk their car horns for you to move out of their way before you get hit or ran over by a car on that busy highway? Whether we like it or not, with or without you change always occurs.

All of us have witnessed people resist or create change. Governments and political parties fight for agendas to be enacted or halted. Technology continues to make last year's new gadgets this year's discount items. Religious authorities and denominations represent the very essence of change as doctrinal philosophies and beliefs conflict creating more new doctrines and denominations. Racism, sexism and segregation were once blatant and legal but today both are subtle and laws exist to protect victims.

With your new power mindset, change now means that no matter what occurs, good or bad, nothing is ever finished but only in transition. No matter how quickly or slowly transition takes place, movement creates vulnerability because of incompleteness during change. As anything changes, the transition presents you with opportunities to exert influence.

In boxing, when a fighter throws a jab or punch towards a competitor the goal is to strike the opponent. The other boxer must move to avoid being hit, attempt to block the incoming punches or counterpunch to offset the aggressor's attack. The boxer under attack is forced to take one or all of the previous actions.

An unprepared, overmatched or cowardly fighter would be defeated easily and possibly knocked unconscious. However, a fighter that embraces the true meaning of change sees an opportunity to counter attack an opposing foe. Whenever a boxer attempts to hit another fighter an opening to be hit is the result. The best fighters know how to counterpunch under attack by opponents.

Being an effective counter puncher requires a fighter to keep poised, absorb punches while delivering counter strikes. To understand the dynamic culture of change you must adopt the mindset of a good counter puncher. This means you can no longer close your eyes, run or resist the tides of change. Instead, look for openings to exert your own attack. Find your power strands and pull them with purposeful intent.

Forget about stopping change. Don't try and avoid it. Don't let shifts overrun you either. Accept adjustments in a way that is advantageous to your agenda. Or plan to wake up the next day with a concussion to ask the person standing over your bed, "What in the world just happened to me? How did I get here?"

Change is your ally. Use it. Transition means opportunity the way attack means counter attack. When circumstances and obstacles threaten your path, see the openings in your opponents and enact your own counter attack to influence the outcome.

Do not let unfavorable odds intimidate your will to locate and use your power strands. We have all been faced with situations and life circumstances that look too powerful to overcome. Yet embracing change entails realizing that no matter how influential or traditionally powerful established circumstances, thoughts, ideas, laws of society and ways of life may appear to be: nothing is ever complete. Nothing is invincible. Change is always a possibility. Remember, power never ceases to exist for you to grasp.

Change is an eternal process. There is no end, only transitions into varying phases of new and revised truths. Some phases of change take longer than others, giving longer transitional phases the appearance of completeness or finality. All forms of tradition are slow to deviate. But don't let the illusion of permanence deceive you. Traditions can fool many who forget, misunderstand or forsake the true meaning of change.

For example, you now know for a fact that the earth is round. But recall how many adventurers and cartographers throughout early history claimed that the earth was flat. Try to envision how many children were raised to believe that ships which sailed too far on the sea fell off the end of the earth. Fathom the lifetimes of people that died not ever learning that our planet was not like a piece of paper. Majority beliefs do not guarantee accuracy or that those who subscribe to such ways of thought will die enlightened.

I know it may sound radical to think that nothing is ever complete, especially in today's so-called modern environment. But if you do your own historical research you'll find that what you presently consider primitive was probably once a religion, law or way of living for generations before you. Unfortunately, every generation makes the mistake of believing in finality.

When hearing your favorite song on the radio, buying that hi-tech gadget or driving the latest vehicle, we sometimes tell ourselves, "It just doesn't get any better than this." Until another song sounds better for another generation, the next hi-tech gadget makes our old gadget obsolete and the latest vehicle makes our favorite car look old and slow. Mankind is in constant transition because we are always learning new things. So don't assume that your present idea of truth will be the last measure of change, it won't.

Imagine how the discoverer of Pluto, Clyde W. Tombaugh, would feel to know that his calculations concerning the planetary status of Pluto made in 1930 are now in our time considered wrong. As a result Pluto is no longer considered a planet but a dwarf object in space. How many of us memorized all the known planets for one of our science exams in school? I'd like to go back and change a few of my science grades and tell my 7th grade teacher that she was wrong for deducting points off my tests just because I forgot to mention Pluto as a planet! But who knows, perhaps the day after this book is released we will learn that Pluto is indeed a planet. I'm not a betting man so I'll stick to writing and public speaking about events on this planet and leave astronomy to the pros.

Knowing now that change is an unending process, understand how it relates to gaining influence. Your situations and circumstances are not final. Change is not always fun, pleasant or wanted, but it's like oxygen: without it, you'd die.

If you embrace change in your life and around you, your ability to adapt and read your situation in order to act accordingly will improve. Variation is only feared because it demands we work to adjust while it exposes that the previous norm is not a good fit for the present reality. Change highlights informative signs that opportunities exist in the forms of surprising allies: obstacles.

The True Nature of Obstacles

Expect them. Know them. Face them courageously. Enjoy overcoming them. Obstacles are reluctant signs of change. They exist to hide or protect the vulnerabilities of opposing factors in your path. But obstructions are really your allies.

When you embrace the true meaning of transition as opposed to fearing new cycles, obstacles become simply agents of change instead of reasons for failures or tools that induce fear.

Think proactively. Since change is ongoing, transitions leave circumstances conducive to the exertion of your influence. Obstacles are only clues that change is necessary and possible. If change were impossible, obstacles would not exist to protect norms.

That means that obstacles are really defensive insecurities of your opposition. Never ignore or underestimate obstacles. Respect them as you would formidable opponents. But do not mistake fear with obedience or subservience.

Fear is natural. Everyone feels it. It signals to us that we are in danger in some way. Unfortunately the feeling of fear is too often misinterpreted as a signal to quit.

Fear is similar to muscles reaching fatigue during weight lifting or lungs demanding more oxygen during running. A body builder or runner can stop working out when muscles ache and fatigue sets in but progression to greater levels of fitness performance will be hindered. Instead the body builder or runner can keep lifting weights or running to expand his or her pain threshold, therefore expanding blood flow to the muscles and air intake into the lungs to enlarge or enhance muscle size and stamina. Athletes call it the "slow burn" and it signals to them to keep pushing themselves if they want to eventually build strength and stamina useful when attempting to perform under pressure and fatigue.

Likewise, your mental and emotional fortitude must be up to the exercises of change. Routine is like the equivalent of a jogger on a treadmill everyday at the same time, for the same duration at the same speed. But if you change the speed, length of time and even incline resistance of the treadmill unexpectedly, you will witness a sudden struggle as the jogger tries to adjust to the changed routine. Since the jogger conditioned his or her body to only deal with one sort of fitness routine, the runner may have difficulty completing the new fitness pattern. You should always avoid longstanding routines which have not produced the results you crave toward your own personal greatness.

If you are ever to obtain power, you must prepare your entire being to be flexible and fit to deal with the dynamic nature of change. Meaning that instead of gearing yourself up to fit in or follow the path most taken, stretch the stamina of your entire being for the highs and lows of transition. Much like a long distance runner prepares for winding roads, hilly surfaces and unpredictable weather. You must understand that obtaining, wielding and keeping power demands you realize your journey is never done. Fortunately, you will have more than one power strand at your disposal to cope with the unending processes of change.

Many paths of influence exist but your vision must pinpoint the transitional opportunities of change suited to your agenda. Fear impulses are merely signals that a higher level of mental and emotional stamina is required to complete the task at hand. To fear pain, failure or resistance is to fear the responsibility of pulling your own power strands to exert influence. Power is not for the cowardly.

On the other hand, respect demands that you acknowledge the influence of obstacles. Though you may not like obstacles or agree with their presence, obstacles have power. Do not underestimate your reluctant allies. Pinpoint, study, understand and respect obstacles. To not do so, is foolish, disrespectful and exposes immature arrogance.

Imagine if a politician never studied current issues affecting the population that votes to put leaders in power. Visualize a prosecuting or defense attorney that never prepares for trial. What would students experience in a class taught by an unprepared instructor?

Ignorance is the compatible mate of arrogance and failure is their love child. Gain knowledge of the obstacles hindering your agenda. Eight major forms of obstacles exist. Know and understand them well. Only then will you be able to find your power strands during change to utilize reluctant allies.

Obstacle 1: Tradition

Tradition is the most deceptive of all the obstacles of change you will encounter. It is like a mountain that seems to have existed well before human life itself. Tradition is the step father of those orphaned by the sometimes slow process of change.

Doctrine, rules, established beliefs, habits and even laws all relate somehow to the concept of tradition. Tradition is "the usual," "the way things have always been." It is the status quo that creates comfort, stability and even glorified monotony.

At times, tradition can even equal the moral equivalent to what is considered right or wrong. If tradition represents the favored child destined to inherit the blessings of the elders, then change is definitely the bastard spotted sheep reluctantly adopted. Yes, tradition has the power and influence to mold generations of thought and action. Representing a way of life for many, once established tradition accepts change the way oil absorbs fresh water.

Sometimes the dynamic nature of change just doesn't arrive fast enough. At times, transitional phases are so slow or appear impossible under the current reality that tradition adorns the illusion of permanence and even perfection. As a result, tradition delivers such a convincing portrayal of finality that anything deviant of the norm is dismissed as nonsense or sometimes scrutinized bitterly. If you want power, prepare to deal with the hierarchy and godlike stature of tradition.

Traditions of all forms gained power by consistently proving worthwhile to many people over a long period of time. For example, when you drive in America you obey traffic lights. Traditionally, red means stop. Yellow means do not enter the intersection (or speed up for the daring that feel there's room for interpretation). Green means go.

Yet imagine if one day you woke up, got dressed, drove your car to the nearest intersection to find that the traffic lights suddenly no longer existed. What would happen? What would you do?

After the initial shock wore off from the missing traffic lights, you'd still have to drive. Traffic jams might occur, accidents might take place and chaotic driving conditions would no doubt plague your route. Drivers would need to use their own judgments to know when to go, stop, turn, merge or yield to fellow drivers. No doubt the individual personalities and decision-making tendencies of each driver on the road would contribute to the overall success or failure of the flow of traffic.

The point is, traditions begin slowly and end even slower for a very powerful reason: if tradition is snatched away suddenly, chaos results as people try and figure out how to think and behave appropriately to deal with the new set of circumstances. Tradition keeps things moving at a steady pace. It ensures that ways of thought and codes of behavior prevail over chaos. People prefer tradition to remain safe and orderly.

Not all traditions are wrong either. As we all know, having a system of traditional traffic laws and lights keeps us all safe, most of the time. That is why you should respect tradition.

Remember, at some point in time tradition served and treated many people well long enough to earn the status of being considered the norm. Typically, tradition has many supporters, agents of influence and hierarchies of power.

Similar to a political opponent with longstanding ties to many communities and wealthy friends in high places, traditions wield muscle and back-up the way kings, queens and presidents keep security and advisors handy. Try calling your country's top leader on the phone. Attempt to walk into the office of your city's mayor unannounced. You'll find that tradition demands things be done a very specific way.

Rules must be followed. Processes are in place. Tradition must be managed properly and efficiently. Why?

Protection and preservation keep traditions alive. The more layers of support and protection, the longer traditions can dominate. Whether religious beliefs, political affiliations or the family get-togethers at your relative's home during holidays, things must be done specifically to preserve and protect customs.

But what happens when tradition no longer satisfies you? When the norm just doesn't work for your life? What do you do when tradition can't answer your questions anymore and represents an obstacle that must be overcome to achieve your own fulfillment?

If you find yourself asking those questions at some point in your life it is time for a change. What's occurring inside you is a lack of fulfillment with your current state of circumstances. Your Inherited Self and Natural Self are not in agreement.

Before change is fully experienced, often people inherit life situations from authority figures, family and society. Once we can no longer function happily in our inherited realities due to personal growth, we must either reluctantly succumb to the norm or change our reality.

Since this book is the average person's guide to power, reluctantly succumbing to the norm is not what I suggest. Take on the change. Create your new reality.

Whatever the situation is that hinders your rise to power, understand the reality first in order to learn how to transcend it. If tradition is your current opponent you must study its origins. Every tradition has a beginning and much to the dismay of those responsible for the illusion of permanence- all traditions have an end. Consider any fallen empire.

No movement or tradition is flawless. Search the beginnings of many current belief systems and traditions that plague your mission to power and you will find flaws, weaknesses that are often hidden. Many unflattering secrets also dwell behind veils of tradition too. Those flaws are your power strands.

It takes a discerning eye, courage to dare ask "why" and poise to meticulously study and expose weaknesses in the obstacles of your upward path. So fear cannot hinder your judgments. You will need a clear head to decipher important issues and circumstances demanding your attention.

To beat tradition, lies must be exposed, flaws highlighted and alternatives presented. Don't take on tradition until you can prove that you know a better way. Otherwise you'll be squashed like a meaningless insect.

Protectors of tradition have much at stake. Money, reputations, credibility, and even your safety can be threatened when you defy tradition. Great victories carry the baggage of great risks. Be prepared.

Obstacle 2: Competition
Competition proves that change is possible. Do not despise competition. Competition contains telling signs. The existence or lack of competition discloses the possible value of your agenda and goal.

If you want something that everyone else wants as well, it's safe to assume that what you want has some value. If you want something that no one else wants, perhaps you're a fool that is deceived or a visionary ahead of your time. Your outlook on power and change coupled with your talent for successfully exercising your power strands will determine if you're a fool or a visionary.

Know your competition well. The forms of competition mimic the possible paths of change. The forces that win create new truths.

You must decide how to maneuver to empower your truth. Your overall goals versus the goals of your competitors dictate which method you should use to win. You can strategically join, defeat or avoid competition. Choose wisely.

Specifically, three sorts of competition exist: weaker; equal; and stronger competition. Each type presents unique challenges.

To always ignore your competitors is foolish. Don't make this error. Many think ignoring competition is a sign of power and maturity, especially when the competition appears not even close to posing a threat to your position or campaign to power. That attitude is nothing but elitist snobbery. Study and respect all forms of competition.

Weaker Competition
Before you dismiss an apparently weaker opponent, see if there is value in your competitor's position. Remember, if you want something that no one else wants, perhaps you're a fool that is deceived or a visionary ahead of your time. Your competitor could be a budding visionary that lacks resources but is on to something you haven't even thought of yet.

If you see promise in the agenda of weaker competition, look for crucial similarities with your own plans. If possible, join them, lead them and benefit in partnering. I call this a "friendly takeover."

Your own cause then secures support from an underestimated, dismissed competitor early. You then have the chance to control and eventually conquer the brewing movement of your competitor at their weakest stage. This will diversify your efforts. Waste nothing, even a weaker opponent.

However, if your competitor is a fool destined to fail because of an inaccurate, weak agenda- ignore flawed distractions. Wait for your competition's demise. Allow your competition to fail in order to highlight the strength of your own campaign to power. Just know that even failures are worth something.

Once your competitor fails, you will witness an opportunity to add to your diversified agenda by recruiting a fallen foe into your plans as you see fit. Or you can discard your fallen competitor and concentrate on more game opposition. Most of the time you will leave a fallen foe as is.

When other competitors witness failure they either re-evaluate their own goals, change their plans or keep steady toward their agendas. Your competitor's failure will lessen competition and make your most formidable opponents known to you.

Influence is gained through the failure of your opponents so your power strands can be pulled to gain even more leverage to position yourself better. However, you will need all the leverage you can get. Obstacles gain even more power when your competition fails. Though you'll have less competition, the roadblock ahead sees your competition fail and wishes or even expects you to do the same.

Equal Competition
You know it when you see it. It's like looking into a mirror or meeting another version of you. Though no two people are exactly alike, you may encounter competition that is just as talented, insightful, ambitious and capable as you are.

Sometimes equal competition has the exact same goal and agenda as you do with equal resources. Don't be threatened. Strategic alliances are then possible.

A competitor similar to you can be a strategic ally or useful camouflage. You can align yourself with similar agendas to add validity to your own cause. Keep a watchful eye on equal competitors because if you look even closer, you may find an a way to differentiate yourself in order to gain leverage that gradually gives you an advantage.

Make mental notes of your temporary ally's weaknesses, which may be similar to your own. How did your equal draw the same conclusions you did? Why do they want what you want? Where did they come from? How do they prepare to act?

Those are questions you need to answer about equal competitors. Just because equal foes appear identical to you doesn't mean they are. A slight difference is present. Perhaps their outlook on the situation or their process of preparation is flawed in some way and has not been exposed yet. You can locate this information by sticking closely to them with an intuitive eye. At the perfect time, you can differentiate yourself by exposing your competitor's flaws so your own agenda takes precedence to gain advantageous positioning.

Until the right time occurs, use similar competitors as camouflage to bait blatant opposition to concentrate their efforts on your temporary allies. When the attack occurs, save your ally to create advantageous leverage for yourself in the eyes of your ally. Influence you can use at a later time. Or watch your ally fail as you move to the next level of power, with one less competitor.

However, if you can't partner, then you must sabotage equal competitors with agendas vastly different from yours by overpowering or outsmarting them. Otherwise you will resort to avoiding your opposition. If avoidance will still get you what you want, then dodge crossing paths with a competitor to save energy. Yet if avoidance is not an option, you must beat your competition. Sounds easier said than done, right? Truth is, sometimes you'll win easily but most of the time prepare for a good fight.

In this case, the obstacle of equal competition demands your best. Commitment to the task should be unwavering. If you're half-hearted in your efforts you are more susceptible to defeat.

Obstacles are not present to make your path to power easy. Don't expect a break or compassion from competitors. Count on opposition aiming to stop you in your tracks. Take nothing for granted as you prepare to face the hurdles of your path.

Beating equal competition consistently means preparation, knowing your gifts and exercising your right to express your truth. What most so-called "losers" neglect to accept is that they have a right to want more. Winners know we have the right to be on top. You know why? To win is to lose the fear of failure.

Fearing failure inhibits effort. Allowing the possibility of not getting what you want to hamper your efforts is to waste energy and lie to yourself. When you don't put your soul into what you do, you are only going through the motions, fooling yourself. Sadly many aspiring winners are really just preparing themselves for failure.

Those afraid to win have built-in "catch phrases" in their minds before they even embark on their quest to win power. "Catch phrases" are psychological comforters that are stored in the minds of people that don't really believe they can win but simply go through the motions of pretending they want power. They know they will bail out of the challenge as soon as the opportunity presents itself. So stored away in their minds are "catch phrases" that catch them when they fall. Meaning they tell themselves things like, "It wasn't meant to be," "Maybe next time," "I didn't want it anyway" or "I don't know what happened."

When facing formidable competition with equal talent, respect your opponent's truth. But know and believe that your truth has just as much right to be in power as theirs. At that point, your mental and physical stamina must outlast your opponent's. To prevail, you must do more than desire power. You must possess power already.

But if you are both equals, how can you have power already? I'll tell you. Have a bigger, better vision than your challengers. The point where all your preparation, knowledge, skill and talent end is where creativity comes in. To imagine is simply to daydream. But to possess vision is to have a long term, creative plan with directions attached on how to get where you want to go!

Imagination is much like a dream. You may understand it, be baffled by it or you may forget it once you awaken. On the other hand, true vision is clear, decisive and instills purpose. You must do more than imagine victory over an equal opponent you must see visions of your conquests that reveal ways to win. No vision? You'll only end up imagining what could have been. Imagination means "if." Vision reveals "how and when."

Stronger Competition

Superior competition poses intense challenges. At first glance stronger competition looks invincible. Seems they may be taller, stronger, faster and smarter. Sometimes stronger competition can be richer, more popular and maybe even better looking! There's nothing worse than looking at stronger foes and wondering, "How in the world did I get into this mess?"

The wisdom in us must then simply admit, "Yes, they are better at what they do than I am. Yes, they are the best anyone can hope to get at what they do. Yes, I have to respect them entirely." However, you must remember one very important thing about encountering stronger competition: they are not you.

Just as stronger competition may be the best at what they do and how they do it. You represent the possibility of change and a new version of truth that just might be superior to even the most admired truth. Just as your stronger foe may be the best in their way of doing things, they are meeting you- the best in your way of doing things.

If you find yourself facing a much stronger opponent you are either a sucker that has been manipulated into a mismatch in order to endure failure for someone else's gain. Or you are more gifted than you accept credit for. The moment you are faced with a stronger foe, you will know inside if you're a sucker or about to be the new dominant reality. The sucker falls easily, as expected. But the new dominant reality wins easily, prevails after a long fight or loses but gains more respect for exposing the vulnerabilities of stronger competition during the long struggle.

In order to have the best chances against stronger competition you must realize that you have as much right to be standing where you're standing as your stronger opponent does. If they're so unquestionably unbeatable, why must they answer to you now? Remember, tradition may be strong but it only gives the illusion of permanence as change is sure to eventually override even the most dominant competition. You must embrace change even more when confronting a stronger foe. In fact, you must be the change that reminds others why those in power must continually prove their worth.

Obstacle Three: Society

Society represents the various phases of change. But it can be a like double-edged sword. In one perspective, it represents order, stability, security and co-existence. On the other hand, society represents organized chaos bordered by goodwill, laws, money and military power.

Both outlooks depend on a basic psychological hold that generates cooperation from people. This mental hold instills a sense of obligation and security in each of us which is derived from flawed, but necessary systems of varied philosophies. The basic psychological hold is: all human beings care about outcomes.

Caring is the primary factor in everyone. Let me be clear. I do not mean the sort of caring like a nurturing parent gives to a child. I am referring to human beings caring about outcomes for selfish reasons, social concerns or both. Even when we do not care for or about others, at the very least self-interest awakens the caring impulse we all have when good or evil outcomes are possible.

A humanitarian cares about homeless people getting shelter and food. A hardened criminal cares about committing offenses against society. Both examples show that individuals care about outcomes but for different reasons. Perhaps the humanitarian cares enough about outcomes related to feeding and providing shelter to the homeless because it makes him or her feel good to help the disadvantaged. Maybe the hardened criminal cares about committing offenses against society because he or she wants to succeed at violating laws to fulfill selfish motivations. Good or evil, outcomes take place and people care about the impacts of occurrences for diverse reasons. Yet caring is always at the core of human motivation.

Society affected you beginning with your family. Your inherited perception of society created your inherited self. The perceptions you have of society and yourself are the psychological and sociological influences that keep you socialized.

What keeps someone from running a red light? What stops us all from going into a bank and demanding as much money as we want? What makes us set up schools, teach, learn and graduate into workplaces that demand certain qualifications, skills and behaviors from us? Why don't we all just do whatever we want, whenever we want, however we want to whomever we want? I'll tell you- we all care about outcomes.

Without the psychological hold of caring about outcomes, human beings would not value life and goodwill, law and order, or systems of justice. Society would always be chaotic. The very concept of society demands that we all care about something.

We care about what happens in our lives and hopefully those around us. So we each respond to caring by fulfilling various responsibilities and roles. We care enough to keep living. We care enough to pursue our interests and make a living. We care enough to operate within society's framework or completely against it.

When society's demands fail people or they can't satisfy societal norms, bad things can happen. Crimes, social injustices, civil wars and international disputes can occur. Unfortunate acts by humans that are evil, unfair or malicious even take place. Shockingly, even the most unthinkable injustices against humanity are based on caring. Even caring has a negative side. For instance, a murderer or rapist victimizes the innocent. Why? Because such twisted individuals care too much about achieving the outcomes of their own selfish motivations. Unfortunately dysfunctional or malicious people do not always positively cope with the pressures of caring about outcomes. So twisted logic and psychological sicknesses exist among us. This does not justify evil, but it does help explain how caring so intensely about outcomes can overwhelm the human psyche.

The underlying primary motivation in every human being, even the worst of us, is the desire to live life in a way that matters in some way. Everyone wants to make an impact and avoid being remembered for nothing. Unfortunately some of us care so much about our own life's outcomes that we resort to being selfish and evil out of fear of becoming nothing in the eyes of others.

Envision a world where human life is not valued at all. What if no laws existed? What would happen if there were no monetary system? What if people worked in order to see the beneficial outcomes of labor instead of the benefits and privileges of money? How would society be without even the slightest threat of violence and warfare?

Such truths can only exist in movies or depictions of heavenly realms in books or pictures. This world is our present reality. We all care about life for many reasons. So much that we will go to great lengths to protect life even while the threat of losing life can be used by all of us to control the living. Societal boundaries regulate the positive and negative extremes of caring.

Human goodwill can inspire us to create laws that promote fair treatment and encourage behavior conducive to overall safety. Laws are written testaments representing our efforts to protect what is cared for. Money is a form of payment and gesture of caring that attempts to symbolize value. Military power is the forceful declaration of intent to demonstrate physical violence to protect or enact what is cared for. Though we all may care about different things for various reasons, we all care about something. This means we all show how we care in unique ways.

What does the underlying societal motivation of caring have to do with gaining power? Society itself is based on caring about outcomes. As you enact your agenda to gain power, know why societal obstacles in your path care enough to exist. If you know why those obstacles care enough to exist, you will know to what extent you must care enough to desire and impose change.

Obstacle Four: Family and Friends

Family and friends represent the past while revealing just how necessary change is for us to live beyond our comfort zone. But some family and friends may want to hinder your growth only to protect you from the harm or disappointment of failure due to change. Sadly, family might want to see you fail to validate their own successes or lack of. Some simply want to use you.

Your failure could please your family because your success forces them to take responsibility for their own shortcomings. Caring less about anything that concerns you is not above family. Though they may wish the best for you, your family and friends have limits to their vision of just what you are capable of. You will witness the boundaries of those limits once you show signs that are unfamiliar to their idea of who you really are or should be in their eyes.

Family and friends possess the power to propel you into the stars, drag you into the depths of hell or keep you locked in the doldrums of mediocrity. Since we are born into our family situations and adopt trusted friends throughout life, we all have "soft spots" for beloved family and friends, sometimes to a fault. Frequently family and friends think they know you so well that they can tell you what is best for you. Your own opinion on what is best for you can even be challenged by family and friends as they attempt to prove to you they know you "better than you know yourself."

Mom and Dad raised you so they think they know how you are. Brothers and sisters know your secrets from Mom and Dad. Best friends know things your own family may not. Everyone you know is familiar with parts of your being. Still, no one knows all of you, except you. Ironically, sometimes we don't even know as much as we should about ourselves.

In relation to power, your family and friends can hinder your rise if they do not share your vision. I'm sure you've witnessed people still dependant on their family's approval in order to feel successful. You may even know people that have never transcended their inherited selves still attempting to fulfill the requirements imposed by their families. So when your vision is not shared by those around you expect to deal with distractions, negativity and skepticism. Do not underestimate the effects of your inherited self on your family and friends.

Your inherited self is the persona given to you and molded by your family and friends while you were young and impressionable. Once you start asking more questions, challenging opinions and defying authority of family and friends you begin the process of establishing your true, higher self. Frankly, people get used to having things their way very easily. Family and friends are no different. If you're always the shoulder to lean on, the reliable one, the black sheep or the favorite, to abandon or expand what they expect of you will cause friction in some way.

If those closest to you can't picture you differently than they perceive you to be, prepare for obstacles. Expect to observe fear, doubt or even indifference in the eyes of family and friends after you share your vision or plans to pursue your dreams. Though you'd desire votes of confidence, emotional support and maybe even financial contributions- don't be surprised if the opposite results. Going against or beyond what family and friends have already imagined for you can be an obstacle influencing your self-esteem, motivation and confidence if you don't outgrow your inherited self. When people come to expect certain things from you, upsetting their expectations can be unsettling. Like a spoiled child used to having things his or her way, family may look you in the eyes to ask you, "What do you mean you're different? What's wrong with you? You never act this way!"

In all fairness, family and friends are a blessing too. Some people are fortunate enough to have family and friends that always seem to come through in difficult, transitional times. To me, everyone should be so lucky. Communal support from family and friends makes for stronger societal values and more defined, united cultures.

Admittedly, some of us are not born into strong or supportive family structures. Abandoned or abused children can experience the unfortunate disadvantages of starting life as outcasts or victims of failed communal ties. Molested, psychologically and physically abused children bear the unfair burden of getting caught in the twisted predatory cycles of people full of self-hatred and dysfunctional addictions. Our world has an underworld of failed dreams and living nightmares which truly displays the extremes of love's absence. Who would think that child abuse or exploitation would ever have a place in this world?

That is why every human being should have family and friends that care. Do not shy away from expanding your own concept of family to include those that are not genetically related to you. In this world, a sympathetic, caring family member or friend is a welcome safe haven at times. Though family and friends can be obstacles to your rise to power, don't think for a second that the concept of family and friendship is a necessary evil. Family structure and friendship is a beautiful, powerful force when embraced and demonstrated in true love.

Your challenge lies in putting the emotional and spiritual attachments of family and friends into a perspective that does not dominate your thoughts and behaviors in such a way that you stop growing as an individual. Eventually you must decide your own path, which may differ drastically from your family history or circle of friends.

Influential plateaus are not accessed without some form of sacrifice. You may lose friends along the way to your realm of power. The worst or most unexpected drawbacks can emerge from your family ties at times when you feel you are finally moving forward. Unfortunately, your closest family ties simply may not understand your vision the way you do.

It's not even fair of you to demand family and friends to see what you see. They are not responsible for your life's outcome after you realize your own power over your existence. Your point of separation from your inherited self represents family and friend's point of ignorance. It's up to you at that point to usher family and friends into your new truth if you see fit.

Obstacle Five: Lack of Resources

A lack of resources means that change is mandatory. We all deserve to have what we need to do what we are capable of. Unfortunately, you will not always have what you need to gain power. Even worse, others will be privileged even if undeserved.

Life is not fair. Deal with it. Just remember: it is completely your choice alone as to how you respond to occurrences and circumstances.

In life, change is frequently imbalanced at first as powers struggle for leverage. Do not expect fairness. Only expect forms of compromise that mimic fairness for spans of time long enough for people to get what they can get while the getting is good. Once the well is dry again, expect more cries and fights for the illusion of fairness to return.

Perhaps you are treated poorly because you're a woman; a minority; from a maligned part of town; a foreigner; a mentally challenged individual; a college or high school dropout; from a poor family; a convicted felon; or a homeless person. Maybe you're not as smart in school or business as others.

You may live in housing projects, rundown trailer homes or in a house with more family members than the local shelter has transients. The school you attended wasn't a private school and was possibly in the poorest part of town. Maybe you're the first in your family to seriously want to achieve something great.

We all know that our societies contain socioeconomic disparities that keep generations of people in negative cycles of perpetual failure due to lack of resources. Lack of education, lost opportunities, crime and poverty creates the ugly side of economics. Wealthy, privileged or even middle class people have chances in life that devalued, poor and maligned people may not ever get or discover. A harsh truth that exists in this world is that someone will die thinking they had no chance to ever accomplish better in life.

As tragic as this reads: imagine someone committing suicide. Picture a human being so distraught their only resolve is to end their own life. Hopelessness is a murderer.

If you feel you lack the resources to defy your circumstances and rise to power, hopelessness has crept into your vision. If hopelessness can snatch a life, imagine what it does to those who are willing to accept living to die. Visions of power fade, a slow process of defeat takes over the mind and people suffering from hopelessness settle for what they can get out of life. Some even become dream assassins that inevitably crush or discourage the hopes of other dreamers.

Yes you may lack money, education, positive support from family and friends. Sure you don't have a car or job. You may not have a bucket to drop a tear into. But guess what? You still have power at your fingertips.

Face your reality: your path may be longer and more difficult than others around you. Your journey may be rockier than everyone you know because of your personal circumstances. You may even be at the bottom of every possible list known to mankind. Yet I say again, you have power.

At every layer of existence is a hierarchy. Whatever crust of society you dwell in, aim to climb to the top of that layer in order to have a better chance to enter the next level of existence. I'm not saying become a predatory social climber. What I mean is for you to always ask yourself, "How can I maximize my time at this level in order to get to the next?"

Similar to a person born into the most negative reality rising to become what no one else thought possible, wherever you now dwell you can elevate your status if you embrace power's unending presence. If you fall into the mindset of those around you controlled by the negatives of the realm you are in, you will become a predictable product of your environment- a living stereotype. The same endings as the ones before you that failed to transcend their circumstances will be yours as well.

Obstacles and circumstances have as much influence and power as your will and desire provide. When you can no longer see possibilities to obtain power, once your will and desire subside, at that point obstacles and circumstances empower excuses and inflate fears. As your visions fade, so does your power.

A lack of resources simply means that you must be inventive, dynamic and crafty to get what you need to climb out of disadvantaged situations. Don't have a car? Stay fit by running and exercising, you may be using your two feet more than the person driving by in a nice luxury vehicle.

Don't live in the best neighborhood? Make sure you take care of what is yours, venture outside your surroundings often and remember there is another world outside of what you see, hear and experience in your neighborhood.

Can't afford to attend a top school? Make the most of where you attend classes by getting the best grades, joining productive extracurricular activities, researching what students at better schools are studying and going to the library to get extra books to read on your own. Can't afford to buy books or a computer? Go get a public library card and use every resource you can get your hands on within that library system. Be proactively resourceful and you'll be pleasantly enthused at the results as you find yourself competing against people that supposedly came from more prestigious paths of life than you did. It matters not where you are from, but how you end up where you are.

Hustle. Understand it. Respect it. Hustle is the average person's ace in the hole. The ability to turn nothing into something requires you to know how to do more with less.

Discipline, ingenuity and persistence are the foundation of any legitimate hustle. Most people reading this book are probably aware of their current status in society and want more. Or some of you are right at the edge of obtaining access to what you've always wanted and want to know how to get over that final hump. You must understand your hustle.

Unfortunately, the word hustle is often associated with trickery or dishonest behavior. I'm not advocating that you lie or break the law. But I am encouraging you to get in touch with your own personalized hustle.

This means not only preparing and demonstrating your best, but finding creative, effective ways to generate opportunities for yourself. If you're waiting on your big break you may as well play the lottery and hold your breath. Good luck.

Sure, every now and then big breaks happen to people who get to experience being in the path of changes favorable to their agenda. Luck doesn't discriminate either. At times the most undeserving people get to ride a wave of good fortune. In luck's case, it's a blind, indifferent force that could care less about you.

Though people like to feel special when luck shines on them, the fact is they were just in the right place at the right time and prepared to capitalize. To hustle is to take more risks conducive to getting caught in luck's path or to create your own favorable outcome.

Savvy instincts and clever strategic moves should characterize every aspect of your hustle. Sometimes the traditional means are not enough to get what you want and you must think outside the lines originally drawn for you. Fitting a square inside a circle can be done, if you expand the circle or shrink the square.

The average person's hustle logic interprets "no" as "try another angle." As with any hustle, order and methodical formulas are hardly the first priority. Getting things done, improvising and turning negatives into positive outcomes are what count most. You may lack resources but never get caught lacking appreciation for the resources you have already. Opportunities for change can manifest in the most unusual, unexpected ways.

Obstacle Six: Lack of Self-Esteem

Low self-esteem is much like being intoxicated beyond reason or under the influence of illegal drugs. Your perception of reality and yourself is warped. You are more susceptible to influences you'd never accept or encounter in your sober, sane state of mind.

Failure, lack of encouragement or poor guidance and bad influences contribute to low self-esteem in people. Even negative past experiences and unresolved destructive feelings add to the stronghold of this unfortunate hang-up. What makes low self-esteem such an elusive problem is it takes on many forms and manifests itself in countless ways all detrimental to decision-making and change.

An extremely arrogant person that exhibits a seemingly flawless, confident demeanor could be hiding low self-esteem. An attractive person with many admirers or plenty of money and success could be concealing low self-esteem. Powerful authority figures or influential mentors with loyal fans or followers are not immune to having low self-esteem. Witnessing low self-esteem by way of family and friends can even create cycles of failure and poor outlooks that pass from one generation to the next. If hopelessness can murder by way of suicide, then low self-esteem is like a brutal interrogator that uses any means necessary to break the psyche.

Similar to a migraine headache, nagging injury or infected wound, lack of self-esteem slows you down and hinders your concentration level at the most inconvenient times. Just when you think you've surpassed vulnerability by preparing yourself. Overlooked issues related to low self-esteem can creep into your agenda and disrupt your progress.

Are you still upset about something that happened to you in the past? Do you still have insecurities about your level of intelligence or attractiveness? Have the negative words of others or memories of failure ever made you doubt your own ability when you need faith the most? Do you constantly have to remind yourself to think more of yourself?

To answer yes to any of those questions reveals that parts of your self-esteem hold vulnerabilities. We all have insecurities related directly to our self-esteem. As soon as you approach the realm closest to your goal, you can count on your self-esteem getting tested. If there are vulnerabilities, you will get exposed unless you solidify your confidence legitimately.

Arrogance, vanity or a condescending attitude- all smokescreens used to hide low self-esteem. Anytime someone needs to emotionally hinder or destroy another person their own self-esteem is in great pain. No one can legitimately establish confidence and healthy self-esteem through arrogance or vanity.

Your self-esteem should be based on your truth not the opinions, ideas or images of others. If you always felt the way other people think you are or look, we'd all be in trouble as personalities and beauty have as many definitions as the meaning of life. Take this to the bank and tell them to double your interest on what you are about to read: do not ever let someone else's problems become yours.

I don't mean ignore the sick, disregard the poor or despise the mentally challenged. What I mean is, don't let someone else's negative conclusion about you become your conclusion as well. Never let someone else's reality affect your self-esteem or you assist the resistance against change.

Obstacle Seven: Lack of Knowledge
The existence of a lack of knowledge at times means that one agenda dominated another agenda so much that information was kept away from those less powerful. People experience a major imbalance in knowledge due to missed or stifled opportunities in education and learning opportunities. What you lack in knowledge

is the difference between the potential for change versus change itself.

Knowledge is more than power as even those that have power must continue to seek knowledge. Without knowledge, wisdom ceases to be possible because knowledge is the infant stage of mature enlightenment. In essence, knowledge is a declaration of intent to become wise.

Know yourself or others will define you. Lead or expect to follow. Decide your path or someone will decide it for you. To decide your path, know yourself or lead, you will need to obtain knowledge.

I will not try to define knowledge the way you typically read it in a dictionary. Knowledge in one realm could be useless information in another. An auto mechanic may possess knowledge of a car's engine but when placed in a chemistry lab to do what a research scientist does, the mechanic is at a serious disadvantage.

Knowledge takes on endless forms depending on where it is most useful. We've all heard of the genius that can't tie their own shoes or the corporate mogul that can't work a computer. Even at the greatest levels of success, people still have weaknesses and lack of knowledge in areas. What this means is that you must obtain knowledge absolutely essential in the area you want to excel in.

Some of you want to skip the basics. Collecting the rewards and praise is easy, but expect to pay dues before your big break. Gaining knowledge is part of preparation. To lack knowledge is to squander opportunities.

Putting your time in, paying dues, doing the little things is part of gaining knowledge and appreciation for your agenda. If you try to convince people you are worth the big bucks but can't prove you embody the necessary temperament nor have the knowledge- you'll be seen as a phony. Securing knowledge related to the path of your agenda means learning the basics, the shortcuts and the alternative routes to your goals. Seeking and absorbing the knowledge related to your agenda will give your passion and emotions attached to your ambition legitimacy.

Self-awareness and understanding is knowledge. Classroom "book smart" knowledge is valuable. "Real world" knowledge shows maturity. "Street smarts" ensures instincts are in place to avoid being naïve and too dependent on "book smarts" and "real world" practicality. Secure many forms of knowledge to give yourself the best chance to utilize your abilities.

Grasping knowledge is part of preparation as you will add to your ability to think and execute under pressure. Often people panic under duress when they simply do not know what to do about the challenges at hand. Though knowledge won't always help you keep your nerves, it can increase your chances of actually knowing where to begin collecting your senses when trials emerge.

Perhaps the greatest reward of having knowledge is the advancement into wisdom. Unfortunately, those with knowledge do not always have wisdom. What this means is that sometimes people don't know how, when or why to use the knowledge they have. So do not underestimate or dismiss the value of learning from mistakes. To oversimplify, a wise person is really just a reformed screw-up with good stories to tell and the uncanny ability to turn negatives into positives.

Imagine a talented chemist that resorts to using knowledge to create illegal drugs that destroy lives. Picture a talented athlete that instead of ending up playing professional sports lands in jail assaulting other inmates. Visualize a beautiful, articulate woman fit to be an international diplomat for peace ending up a homeless prostitute instead. Knowledge takes on many forms but without wisdom, one can end up in the most unfortunate situations.

Wisdom means utilizing information in ways that exhibit knowledge ahead of one's time. Patience, tactfulness and positive results are signs of wisdom coupled with functional knowledge. A fool can know it all, but a wise person knows better.

Obstacle Eight: You

Your mental outlook can and will make or break your chances for success. Why is your life the way it is now? Do you believe in destiny? Do you believe in fate? Do you believe in good and bad luck? What is your belief and value system?

Your answers to those questions unveil your mindset. How you interpret the reasons for your current status in life determines whether or not you will decline, stay the same or excel. The state of mind you live by influences your thoughts, actions and reactions. All the advice, assistance and chances granted to an individual operating in life under the wrong frame of mind will prove fruitless eventually.

If you are operating with a mindset handed to you by those before you but are experiencing internal conflict as to how you should execute your agenda to accomplish your goals, chances are you need a mindset makeover. If you are consistently not satisfied with outcomes in your life something is wrong. What worked for your family, friends and associates may not work for you. Perhaps your vision demands a more unique mindset tailored more specifically to fit your vision.

I often ask people, "Do you believe in destiny?" Most respond, "Yes." The word "destiny" is the prettier version of the word "fate." Both words are associated with predetermined outcomes. If an outcome is predetermined then no matter what actions are taken or avoided beforehand, the results are inevitable. Though change is a predetermined truth, it is the nature of outcomes that you can have a part in. In other words, good or bad outcomes are not predetermined.

For example, visualize a little boy about five years old that shows great skill with building blocks. When the little boy becomes an adult, he ends up a famous architect. His family, friends and associates then claim, "He was destined to be a great architect. He was always good at building things."

Now picture a little girl about five years old who can complete college-level arithmetic better than most college students. But when the little girl becomes an adult, she ends up a mental patient in an insane asylum. Her family, friends and associates then claim, "She was always strange. Her mind didn't work like everyone else's. Her diagnosis is not surprising. It was her fate."

The word "destiny" gets assigned to positive predetermined outcomes. The word "fate" is used to describe negative predetermined outcomes. To me, both words are distractions in the search for truth and power. Take careful note of the following: destiny and fate do not exist. Here's why: if predetermined positive or negative outcomes are true, then there is no significance to our choices and actions at all. You should just sit around and do nothing until your fate or destiny finds you. After all, if the nature of the outcome is predetermined then no matter what you do or not, your outcome will occur, right?

Destiny means that even if that same little five year old boy decides never to pick up a pencil and draft his first building he will end up a famous architect. Fate means that no matter what, that five year old girl's mathematical genius will still land her in an insane asylum. To fully believe in either destiny or fate is to hand over all of your own power to external circumstances.

It's similar to standing motionless in the middle of a busy street and getting struck by a car only to say, "It was fate." Or, it's like receiving a chance to take on a really nice job though you have no experience or background in the profession only to say, "This is my destiny."

In our world, we often like to add mysticism to outcomes. When we watch, listen or read about the lives of famous or influential people we often enjoy saying these people were "destined to be great." It sounds powerful and even godlike. It adds extra meaning and legitimacy to positive outcomes when we give destiny the credit for results.

On the other hand, when tragedy occurs, someone is murdered or natural disasters occur, we say things like, "It was fate. It was a fateful day. Fate intervened." We often sensationalize negative outcomes with the word fate. But have we all really considered the meaning and power behind the words we use to describe outcomes in our lives?

Again, why are you where you are in life? Is your current status due to destiny or fate? If you still attribute your present to the past's circumstantial influences, then you have a predetermined outlook on life. People with mentalities committed to predestination are often reacting to life rather than enacting their life's agendas.

Instead, believe more in the power of choice. From the moment you wake in the morning your day begins and ends with your outlook and how you choose to respond to life. Furthermore, I want to stress that you do have a choice concerning how you react to occurrences. Just because your first impulse leads you to respond a certain way does not mean that your reaction will benefit your agenda. Change is a predetermined reality but you have a say in what types of changes take place.

We are all conditioned to respond to certain things in very specific ways. Yet sometimes our conditioned responses are bad habits. Stress may cause you to eat too much, drink liquor or even throw tantrums. Happiness and success may cause you to become lazy or arrogant. If you take a minute to introspectively explore your own actions during heightened moments in time, you'll catch yourself in the middle of a conditioned response.

Ever had to stop yourself from saying something that should not be stated at the time? Have you ever had to monitor your own temper tantrums? During unhappy times, do you have to pay close attention to how you treat your own body? From now on when you wake ask yourself this: Will it be a day that acts on you or a day that you act upon?

I honestly believe that people resort to believing in destiny and fate when they are so overwhelmed by or fearful of reality that they can't imagine themselves taking full responsibility for their life situations and need some other influence to hide behind or blame.

Destiny does not give credit to inherited aptitudes, hard work and persistence for overcoming failure and fighting for success. Your natural gifts are given to you by something greater than yourself. But without developing your gifts, consistently working to exercise your passion and the ability to transcend obstacles, your outcome will be what is handed to you. If that outcome is negative, you can choose to adopt a predetermined outlook and claim it was fate that handed you bad cards. Or you can take responsibility for every choice you have made up until this point and admit that destiny does not mean rewards without hard work. It means hard work that can result in earned blessings.

In regards to fate, negative outcomes occur. Bad things happen to good people sometimes. We all wish that people didn't get struck by stray bullets, die in plane crashes or lose shelter to floods, hurricanes or tornados. As human beings, we all sympathize with innocent victims of violence and natural disasters.

I'm sure you've watched the news and seen a story of someone that experienced something tragic or even lost their life. Sad stories are easy to find in this world. We have all asked ourselves, "What did that person do to deserve that? Why did that happen to such a good person? Why couldn't that person be saved or spared such an awful fate?" I've seen some people count tragic endings as part of some grander scheme to teach the living a lesson. I've watched the relative of a slain child tell reporters, "My child has gone to a better place. This was meant to be. It was their time."

No doubt, death and tragedy happens. But I view negative or sad outcomes, even those that are completely unfair, as harsh realities not predetermined outcomes. A loving family is not fated to lose their home to a flood. A teenage girl is not fated to be kidnapped and raped. A five year old child is not fated to be molested, hit by a car or stray bullet. Unfortunately, these harsh realities take place in our world.

Why? There is a reason for everything, a source of every occurrence. You may not like or appreciate the process of every outcome, but your disdain does not alter the truth. We live in an imperfect world where things can and will go wrong at times despite our best wishes, intentions, plans, efforts and precautions. Even negative happenings are simply processes of life.

Luck does exist, but not how we have always believed it to be. Luck is really the results of processes intersecting at times when we are in heightened states of awareness. During escalated sensitivity to our surroundings and personal awareness, happenings take on greater significance to us.

Imagine being in dire need of cash. You are about to be evicted from your apartment if you do not pay $1000. Stressed, you go for a long walk and find $1000 on the ground at a park you have never visited before until that day. Most would say you encountered really good luck.

On the contrary, what if that previous scenario did not end with you finding $1000 dollars to pay your rent? Instead, when you get to that same park, you're mugged by someone that finds that you have no cash at all. So you're shot in the leg and almost bleed to death before an ambulance arrives. Then you get stuck with a medical bill for the treatment you received but you have no money to pay that bill either. Especially since the main reason you fell behind on your rent was because you lost your job and health insurance benefits. Most would say you have "bad luck."

I like to refer to the belief in luck as "wind logic." If you place a piece of tissue outside it will float in any direction the wind blows. Luck is the same.

The $1000 dollars you found in the park was your good fortune and someone else's bad luck. Two intersecting paths created two outcomes that we label "good" or "bad" luck. Luck always creates winners and losers. In a way, luck is one of the purest concepts. It does not discriminate. It does not play favorites. Luck does not judge or condemn.

Ever seen a person you feel is not a genuine or nice individual catch a break in life? Imagine a co-worker that lies and skips out of responsibility at every chance, but still lucks up on a promotion or a better job making more money than you. Have you ever seen an arrogant, condescending and bitter person win millions in the lottery? Luck happens to saints and sinners.

Luck to a sinner is often termed "grace" as people view favor on the unjust as a warning or opportunity for sinners to become better individuals. Luck to a saint is viewed as a reward for faith and good behavior. Luck to the indifferent is perceived as a "sign" to believe in luck. As you can see, how you interpret outcomes determines how you label occurrences.

However, if you rely on luck to get you what you want you may as well get in line and play the lottery with your paycheck. Luck does not really exist exclusively for you. It could care less about how good or evil you are. Luck only cares about one thing: the opportunity to exist. Like the words "destiny" and "fate," the term "luck" is another title applied to outcomes that overwhelm explanation.

Those who experience bad luck consistently, typically have outlooks that believe in predetermined outcomes. People who experience consistent good luck eventually conclude that luck is really hard work, preparation and finally persistence meeting opportunity. It takes more than being at the right place at the right time, you must be aware and prepared to take advantage of intersecting paths of change. Without the proper mindset, you will not be able to cope effectively with obstacles.

A person that works to become a billionaire has a considerably different mindset than someone that is fulfilled with a bi-weekly paycheck, their own cubicle and a company pen. What you expect from your mindset is what life manifests.

Whether the Natural, Inherited or Higher Self, the perceptions and actions you take emerge from one or all of these places inside you. Begin to ask yourself, "What place inside me impacts this outlook or decision the most?" Pinpoint what state of mind you see and act from during your life travels. The mindset you see and live from defines you.

So even if you are not where you want to be in life now, you should adopt the mindset that you are on your way to where you want to be. Remember, change is a predetermined reality but you have a say in what types of changes take place. Balance the influence of your chosen mindset by respecting the inevitability of change as the First Superior Truth will help you take full advantage of the Second Superior Truth expanded on in the next chapter.

Chapter 3: Power

According to the First Superior Truth, change is unending and inevitable. No situation, circumstance or outcome is ever complete. Unfinished outcomes mean that voids exist. Endless opportunities to fill such voids make the Second Universal Superior Truth advantageous to you: power is always accessible.

As endless as the outer solar system is, so is your access to power. Even more exciting is that many forms of power exist. So before you can effectively gain and utilize power an understanding of its meaning and significance is necessary. If not, ignorance wields power like an intoxicated driver maneuvers a car. Expect the worst.

Each of our ideas about possessing power differs based on our beliefs, convictions, ambitions and circumstances. For a poor person, maybe money is power. For a rich person, love with true friendship and happiness could be power. An artist may view freedom of expression as power. Humanitarians may consider power as the ability and means to help others. A business person might see the concept of capitalism as power. So what does power mean to you?

Define it. Establish what you feel represents power in your life and the environments or realms that you wish to excel in. Yet no matter what your idea of power is, one basic premise always applies: power is intangible influences manifested through tangible vessels onto targets to create tangible and intangible outcomes. In short, power makes things happen.

The power of money, politics, religion, sex, violence, love, hate and countless other versions of influences dominate our world. Despite the infinite summations of power, all forms entail the exact same four components: influence, vessels, targets and outcomes.

Influence empowers vessels. Vessels exert influences. Targets adhere or object to influences to produce outcomes. Outcomes are interpreted as good or bad based on various perspectives. The model of power is simple. But mastering the fluctuating dynamics of the four elements is not.

1. Influence

First, influence is the intangible source of all power. It is indirect power, implied dominance. Like air is felt, breathed and exhaled to sustain human life yet never seen, influence is like an unseen force that not only implies power but adds significant presence to any situation. Overwhelming, commanding, soothing, validating or even confusing, influence makes things happen. Your influence must be felt to enact power.

Keeping an outstanding reputation, the ability to instill confidence, inspire dreams, ignite desire or create mystery are examples of unseen yet impactful aspects of the magical nature of influence. Minus influence, power is just a word, a useless concept. Influence adds meaning and significance to outcomes. Power's credibility lies in the nature and perception of magnetism. To establish the type of influence you want, two elements are required: your potential and drive.

First, your potential is created by the possibility of outcomes taking place. Like a friendlier version of a threat, potential's influence has more power over targets when the chance of potential fulfilling itself appears evident. Your potential is like an unplanted seed that if planted, cultivated and nurtured could grow to become a marvelous forest over time.

All around you are influences. A newborn baby influences with the potential for a new future. New opportunities influence with the potential for new experiences. A traffic stop sign influences with the potential for accident-free driving conditions. What you must do is work hard to improve the likelihood of your personal potential blossoming into a reality. If you do, you will not only have influence, you can then transmit the necessary aura or presence that creates the sort of magnetism which empowers your stature.

Ever noticed how people treat you differently when they think you may have an advantage they do not have or potential that appears likely? Imagine how you would be treated if you were holding a winning lottery ticket. Envision the looks on the faces of the parents of a hard-working high school senior that gets accepted into a prestigious university. Potential's power lies in the likelihood of success.

However, if you are ever to harness power in your life, you must be able to at least recognize potential for outcomes. You have to envision opportunities even when the outlook appears desolate. Finding potential means you examine your circumstances to answer a very important question: "Where is my power in this situation?"

Look for power strands. They are the seeds of potential. Nurture your advantages.

Potential is best recognized when you exhibit the will to believe there is always more to be gained. When you search for the power in every situation, you are really attempting to locate possibilities, your opportunities for exerting your agenda. A resourceful mentality always probes for useful, effective ways to win. Your influence is always respected when you remain relentless.

Finding potential means to pinpoint your power in the circumstances then embrace and harness the influences which add potential to your agenda. When you can spot potential in your situation you have executed the very first step in achieving power: finding power strands.

So when you have no money to pay the electricity bill and the fees for your kids schooling is past due, know you still can find your power strands. Sometimes you'll have to look long and hard to find power strands. Admittedly, when circumstances appear bleak sometimes you'll need an extra strength magnifying glass to find a tiny shred of power strands. Still, the key to having a puncher's chance in the dark is to have the nerve to truly explore where your power strands are. If you're afraid to even explore your options and give in to fear or depressing circumstances, you forfeit your outcome to forces around you.

Ironically, influences are limitless in form but limited by your creativity. Influence can be money. Influence can be emotional support. Loyalty from associates or friends can be influence. Depending on what you need to gain advantageous leverage, influences are power strands that partner best with inventive minds.

Similar to being lost or trapped on an uncharted island, you have to creatively explore everything around you to find ways to persist. You'd be surprised how resourceful you can be when your normal comfort zone is gone and you then have to figure out ways to persist. Since influence has endless identities, you are free to explore traditional and nontraditional means of locating your power strands.

Tapping into influences requires that you not fear the process of problem resolution. Obstacles and challenges should only be seen as clues that change is possible. Something needs to be resolved, something must be changed and actions must be taken. In your mind, solve problems by recognizing potential and channeling influences for your power strands. As long as you embrace the inevitability of change, you will always see the potential for influence when creatively reaching for your power strands.

The second part of your influence lies in your persistence. Potential without drive equals lost opportunities. Drive is volition, the relentless intent to persist through all obstacles. When someone looks in your eyes, they should feel your intent and then know one thing: you will not stop until you reach your goal. While recognizing and developing potential is essential, if your drive does not match your level of talent expect to one day sit in a rocking chair telling your grandchildren what could have been if you'd done more.

What differentiates the not-so-average person from the average person is not always intelligence or education, but drive. For instance, you can read this book from cover to cover in less than 24 hours and memorize every word. Yet if you sit on the information, contemplating your agenda, planning your strategy but never make moves to obtain your power then you're an amateur dreamer. I wrote amateur because professionals get paid. Don't you want to be a professional dreamer?

There is always someone out there smarter, richer, prettier, more educated or talented than you. Competition will only increase as younger generations join the fight to gain power as well. Your dream is not just your dream but thousands of others probably want the same.

No one can guarantee you'll get what you want. Even the most gifted individuals fail. In fact, you will fail many times before you get your prize.

So how intense is your drive? How do you respond to failure? Do you quit, change your mind, make excuses and blame others? Do you allow setbacks to make you take a longer time-out than necessary? Do you convince yourself that you don't really want what you failed to acquire? Are your parents or upbringing to blame?

Working hard at working smart originates with your drive. No one can teach you drive. Sure you'll hear a good pep talk or read an inspirational book then feel suddenly invigorated to conquer the solar system. Yet after the adrenaline wears off, the books are closed and back on the shelf, the motivational guru leaves town for the next gig, does your drive subside as well?

Drive is not occasional efforts. Nor is drive exhibiting lukewarm attempts just to say you tried. Trying isn't good enough any longer. Forget the notion that drive means going for it all no matter what, even if you've done no preparation to give yourself the chance to win. Reckless efforts do not validate your desire to succeed, only your lack of respect for the success you claim to want.

Many people want the rewards of power and marvel at others that achieve greatness. If asked, most people will claim they'd love to be on top, in charge, successful, rich or even famous. Lots of middle managers claim to want chief executive status; plenty of actors say they want marquee billing; millions of athletes dream of going pro; countless entrepreneurs speak of wanting successful business ventures. If success isn't guaranteed no matter how much talent, intelligence or education you have, imagine the likelihood of gaining power without drive.

Do you cringe at making sacrifices? Do you put in time preparing to conquer your agenda even when play time rears a smile in your direction? When your competition is asleep are you still at work? Do you jog or run that extra mile even when you are exhausted?

Sure we'd all love to get what we want easily. That's why if you ask any person if they would like to be rich and powerful most will say, "Yes!" It's easy to want something for nothing. But do you have the drive to work through the rejection, setbacks and opposition?

Unfortunately, many average people look at and admire others more successful in such awe that we all sometimes assign godlike status to people who are not much different than ourselves. In admiration, we even ask, "How in the world did they do it? How did they become so good at what they do?"

Sometimes average people will even dismiss any notion within that dares even think of acquiring status equal to or greater than more successful individuals. We all have placed limits on our dreams and ambitions at some point or another. Those that transcend the limits we have imposed on ourselves we admire and hold in great regard. But the truth is, if we never limited ourselves we'd realize that the people we marvel at eat, sleep, drink and breathe like we do. Their crap stinks too, just like yours.

Sure people that secure greatness in life deserve respect. Still, putting success into an informed perspective is what we should remind ourselves to do. Those that eventually get where they want to be do so because they kept trying until they reached their goal. You can do the same with your agenda if you keep your drive and have the skill, talent and ambition to do so. But it starts with recognizing your power strands and nurturing your potential influence with relentless drive. With such intent, your influence will precede even your actions. Others will sense your potential and respect your projected internal drive. The invisible energy of influence can and will ensure that your aura, your presence oozes with the temperament of success. People respect, follow and admire such impact.

2. Vessels of Power

Influence needs vessels to manifest outcomes. You are a vessel. People around you are vessels. Vessels carry out objectives that complete agendas which fulfill missions. Not to seem inhumane, but no amount of influence matters without vessels, the second aspect of power.

Common belief is that power is only witnessed in obvious images of strength and prominence. So vessels great in size or loud in sound frequently carry the stigma of power in the eyes of most people.   Yet power's multidimensional existence is often underrated as even the most desolate looking existences wield power.

Vessels that no one would think to consider influential surround us. To be small in size or meek in speech does not eliminate the likelihood of power. No matter where you're from, what race you are or your gender, you have power.

Again, power is limitless in forms but limited by your personal creativity. So the more vessels you can envision as agents of change and power, the higher your number of power strands will be. The first vessel of power you must acknowledge, embrace and develop is you.

As a vessel, you can channel or be channeled by energy. Energy is the available capacity of influential forces. Think of energy as fuel. At your disposal are three types of energy: negative, positive and neutral.

Negative energy is destructive. Neutral energy invigorates both positive and negative forces. Positive energy is constructive.

To begin, negative energy is a disruptive force that stagnates, distracts or even destroys. There is power in negative energy. Depending on your agenda, negative energy can be either a reluctant ally or obvious enemy.

Negative energy is the easiest to find. Anger, jealousy, maliciousness, deceit, vulgarity and hopelessness are some forms of negativity that will always exist in our world. So powerful is negative energy that poverty, war and murder are in no danger of becoming extinct concepts in our lifetimes and derive from negative energy.

From a tactical standpoint, negative energy can be ignored, absorbed, changed, manipulated or destroyed. Do not ever be naïve in thinking negative energy will not challenge you at some point during your path. When dealing with negative energy you must weigh your options.

Consider the following: if absorbing negative energy does not motivate you to win with positive energy; if changing negative energy into positive requires more energy than the resulting change provides positive outcomes; or if destroying negative energy will only waste your time- you should ignore and avoid negative energy.

However, absorb negative energy as a motivational tactic only when you can maintain your focus, purpose and vision then create positive outcomes. Take note. Success is always the best revenge.

Change negative energy only if you see the benefit of converting adverse forces and have the ability, patience and will to enact a better plan.

Manipulate negative energy when it cannot be ignored and must be diverted onto another target, deceived or lured into stagnation.

Destroy negative energy when it can no longer be ignored, absorbed, changed or manipulated.

Neutral energy is tricky. Like encountering a person that never picks a side or goes where the wind blows, neutral energy lacks direction. Think of a person you know that is indifferent, uninformed or indecisive concerning your agenda. Neutrality is like an empty bottle floating on an open sea.

Interestingly, there is power in neutral energy to be gained. To sway neutral energy your way you must consider that neutrality does not mean ignorance. Neutral energy could be in the process of choosing a side, feeling alienated in some way, or planning to stay objective. Obtain the support of neutral forces by simply offering your very best and attempting to understand why neutrality exists in the first place.

Let's say you have just been promoted and now manage three people. One person accepts your leadership willingly and proves loyal. But the second individual hates that you got promoted over them and intends to make your work life a living hell. Finally, the third person seems indifferent and shows no loyalties to anyone.

You can only do one thing to turn neutral energy into positive energy for you. You must be the clear choice, the logical side to partner with. If you try too hard to sway neutral energy, you'll appear desperate or deceptive. You may even cause the neutral force to feel sorry for or side with your competitor. So remember this, neutrality often favors independent thinking, objectivity and quality.

If your agenda is sound, neutral energy may not support you directly or claim you are the answer, but your opponent's agenda may not be any better off than you in the eyes of neutrality. Extend a willing hand to neutral energy but never force the issue. It's best to sway neutrality your way by just being good at what you do. Chances are, if neutral energy remains neutral, you've already won as your opposition has not gained a new supporter either.

On the other hand, true positive energy should always be absorbed. It is a force that confirms, energizes and can even carry your efforts to new heights. You'll know positive energy from negative energy if you ask yourself one important question: "What could happen if I invite this energy into my life?"

Some energy feels good but only wants to control or exploit you. Some energy looks good but is only a distraction. Fake positive energy always steals from you and gives nothing in return. But true positive energy coincides with your agenda so much that a mutual exchange of giving and taking occurs. When you encounter true positive energy you will end up feeling as if you gave just as much as you received. Call it a mutual exchange.

Harnessing positive forces is like meeting or reuniting with friends and family, you just feel like you belong together. A common mistake by us all is that we sometimes do not fully embrace and absorb positive energy the way we should. Distractions, lack of time and even fear of missing the next opportunity can prohibit us from soaking in positive energy. We must remind ourselves that we deserve to encounter positive forces.

A vacation, a good rest or sleep, a long hard laugh with friends or listening to our favorite music and becoming free of stress- these things remind us that living does not always have to be work and problem-solving. At times, it's good to just enjoy realities as they are and appreciate your own existence. Indulge positive forces.

Laugh at a joke, make fun of yourself, go out and act silly in public sometimes to bring a smile to someone else's face. Look in the mirror and tell yourself, "I'm so good looking I can't stand myself!" Burst into a silly dance around your house then scream, "I'm the greatest!"

Go to a concert, sporting event or parade and scream your head off. Go dancing or to a comedy show. Have fun and don't take yourself so seriously that you have to remind yourself that you're human. Some might even feel a little selfish about purposely taking a time out from responsibility to submit to positive energy. But I'll tell you what I think: sometimes you just absolutely need to think about yourself first.

Children will never stop needing you. Friends will often take as much as you can give of your time. Your job can and will work you to death if you let it.

Problems await you at every turn, especially when you look for new challenges every waking second. To be blunt, sometimes you need to shout, "Forget it all! I'm doing what I want to do now. Anyone who has a problem with it can kiss me where the sun's about to shine while I get a nice tan!" Become the center of the universe for a spell and enjoy it.

Dedicate personal time for yourself to re-energize and appreciate yourself and positive energy. Take compliments with a smile. Let someone buy you lunch. Listen to the standing ovation after your presentation and think to yourself, "That's right ladies and gentlemen, appreciate me while I'm alive." Every now and then, it's good to kiss your own butt.

After all, life won't hesitate to kick you in it again, will it?

3. Targets of Power

As a vessel, with influence you must also interact with other vessels. Vessels are the targets of power. The third element of the power model involves other people.

In life there will always be leaders and followers. The ironic truth about the existence of leaders and followers is that at all times we assume both roles. The balance we maintain between leading and following depends on which level of life's hierarchy of power we operate in during various moments in time.

So if you are the supervisor of a team, you are the leader and they are the followers. But simultaneously you follow the person that manages the entire department. A hierarchy of power exists at all times. Your measure of power versus your obligation to follow means that to effectively exert influence over targets you must relate to the subjects of your agenda that you want to influence.

Ever had a boss that was good at telling you what to do but had no idea how you actually got your job done? If that boss didn't attempt to relate to your reality by at least letting you know they appreciated the concept behind your responsibilities and what you contributed, that leader's influence was only reinforced by their title. Meaning that the only reason you respected that boss was because they possessed the authority to possibly fire you.

No good leader wants to be respected merely because they possess a title of authority. Instead, if you want to harness power and exert influence over targets prepare to earn much more than obligatory respect derived from a title. You must become who you want others to believe you are.

As a kid, I used to enjoy watching pirate movies. I always wondered how a ship full of thieves and criminals remained under control by the ship's captain. After all, couldn't mutiny erupt on a pirate ship at any time considering the rebellious natures of those aboard?

How does one captain rule over a bunch of rogues carrying swords? What stops the other pirates from throwing the captain into the sea? How is order maintained?

Power is much more than a title of authority. Just as targets of your agenda must be much more than subjects carrying out orders. You have to know what motivates and ultimately regulates the beliefs, decisions and actions of those servicing your goals. In addition, you must understand their perceptions of authority in relation to your agenda.

Any good influencer knows that while you can't be everything to everyone, you still must exhibit versatility in your persuasive efforts. For some followers you encounter you will take on the role of coach, mentor, parental figure, disciplinarian or even friend. In the eyes of those you intend to influence you will represent some form of power they are willing to respect and even obey or follow. To not be aware of how you are viewed by those servicing your agenda is to take your power for granted.

Some leaders dictate, others use team building techniques, delegation or even rotate leadership responsibilities between subjects to create a balanced arena of influence. Your style of leadership depends on your perception of authority, your agenda in relation to the circumstances surrounding you and how well you are in tune with the dynamics of your influence. If you truly keep in perspective your balance between following and leading, those that follow you will prefer your leadership. As a result your targets will feel empowered by following you while executing what you need done for your agenda.

Set the stage for your targets. Lead them into situations of success. Exploit their strengths and don't set them up to fail. When you can lead targets into your agenda by offering each target a chance to fulfill their own measure of success more power is the result.

4. Outcomes

Influence empowers vessels. Vessels exert influences onto targets. Targets adhere or object to influences. Outcomes are the final part of the power model.

Success and failure is measured by the consequences of outcomes. Acquiring power to execute your agenda demands that you understand the nature and significance of outcomes since responsibility is great when you wield influence over others. To me, the most incredible aspect about exerting power is the ability to accurately anticipate outcomes.

No one can predict the future accurately all the time, but the most influential and powerful people seem to make the right moves, at the right times to acquire the right results. If done enough times successfully, one may even appear almost prophetic. Anticipation is an instinct that can be used to possibly set up the increased likelihood of desired outcomes.

Simply put, you have the power to interrupt, redirect and even manipulate things around you to achieve your desired endings. Energies stirring about can be harnessed by you and molded into what you need. Remember, you are a vessel that can not only be used by, but can also channel energy as well.

Going back to the premise of chapter one, if you know and embrace that change is inevitable you'll have the inclination to inject your vision of what you want change to be. Since everything around you is in constant transition, you can capture paths of life the way your hands can redirect a stream of water from a waterfall into a cup. That cup should be your anticipated outcome. Have an ending in mind. Even if you must adjust your vision, to have no foresight into the endgame is to leave your outcomes to destiny or fate.

Goals that you set for yourself are really cups waiting to be filled with redirected energy from your hands. Your aspirations are really desired outcomes. Since the model of power begins with influences, progress by way of vessels, is maintained by targets and judged by the nature of outcomes. You have the best chances of creating and predicting outcomes by abandoning the fear of failure.

Most people hate to be wrong. Experiencing failure, unexpected setbacks or opposition convinces many people the comfort of playing life safe most of the time is the best way to live. Honestly, not everyone can be inventive or afford to take risks. That's what makes outcomes so relevant. Most people fear the very nature of outcomes not because they have negative outlooks but because they forget that no outcome is final due to change's dynamic existence.

Do not ever forget this. You should perceive events in your life properly. In regards to any outcome, I always remind myself, "Put it in perspective. It's part of a process." No outcome is final, only part of a larger process.

Processes can be changed or even stopped for a time. What you recognize as a process can also be a power strand. So if your agenda requires, outcomes should be seen as opportunities to cultivate more processes.

Not So Average? Prove It.

Because change is inevitable, the Second Superior Truth is that you always have power in any situation. Your influence by way of your potential and drive makes you a likely vessel for success. People can and will be influenced by you. Outcomes that you desire will result.

But before your agenda is possible, you have to know what you're bringing to the table. Who are you? What do you stand for? What can you do? Once you know yourself, then you'll be able to contend with the fluctuating dynamics of influence, vessels, targets and outcomes. Even as a so-called average person, you have gifts.

Simply put, a gift is a quality that is a positive, reliable characteristic. Consider gifts as aptitudes, inherent and unique qualities humans are born with. Gifts manifest in endless ways and emerge at various phases of one's life. No doubt you've heard at some point in your life that everyone has at least one gift.

I despise that saying because it is false. The truth is we are all definitely born with many gifts. So not only do you always have access to power, multiple talents and skills are at your disposal at all times.

Some discover their gifts early in life. Others uncover their talents after many life experiences teach valuable lessons. So if you are not sure at this point what your gifts are do not be discouraged. Keep living and be open to exploring change and you will surely unveil your talents. Whatever you do, do not subscribe to the belief that we are only born with one gift.

Frankly, much of the failure you witness around you could be due to the fact people neglected to embrace their inherent multitalented natures. One gift is not always enough because the sad reality about this world is that not everyone will discover, harness and exercise their talents to the fullest potential. Nor is there room for everyone with the exact same gifts!

I know plenty of failed actors that never got the big part, athletes that never went pro and inventive minds that banked on one idea that never received recognition. There is nothing wrong with being loyal to a dream as long as you realize you have more than one wish in your lifetime. What makes a fulfilled dream special is the way it reminds us we do not have to settle for less. But what makes success even more rewarding is the way failed dreams remind us that life does not end.

If you're still standing after a failed dream it just means that you are free to keep dreaming. How many people do you know that settled for less? They settled because they dared not dream new dreams, or maybe never had one in the first place.

Therefore, instead of fixating on only one gift you may have, cultivate your other aptitudes as well. Some of you might feel that resorting to developing any other talents other than the one you've banked on being your bread and butter is giving up on your dream. You may even feel that you'd be doing nothing but preparing for failure and copping out with a Plan B.

Narrow minds all have one thing in common: predictability. Don't be predictable by fixating on one of your gifts while ignoring your other aptitudes. Change does not go hand in hand with predictability as set ways usually resist transitional opportunities. You can miss new dreams if you do not creatively recognize all your power strands of influence. One failed dream may open doors to dreams you never thought possible.

Discover your gifts by recalling things you were drawn to as a child that brought you pleasure and fulfillment. As kids, we could not always explain or properly interpret all the influences surrounding us but we were able to memorize feelings. Maybe a certain color made you feel happy or a specific song brought joy to your heart. Even behaviors you can remember doing that no one ever taught you or encouraged you to exhibit, tendencies that just emerged seemingly out of nowhere.

You should try and search your memory for those sorts of pleasant moments as you are now mature enough to relate them to your present actions and preferences. As a very young child, I loved to pick up a pencil and draw pictures of athletes and buildings. As an adult I love basketball, boxing, football and tennis and have played all of them at one point in time. I am not an architect but I adore admiring buildings that exhibit unique structure. Both sports and architecture demand creative problem-solving, a desire to conquer and build, attention-to-detail and meticulous preparation skills- much like writing. I may not have a basketball jersey or skyscraper with my name on it, but I have a book that bears thoughts helpful to those that can relate. You can find your power strands even now because you are born with so many.

Once you pinpoint your gifts, study and cultivate them. Find out how your gifts come to life. Learn as many paths as you can to stage the showcase of your talents. Similar to choosing a field of study in college or a career path, all of your gifts are power strands that require development, practice and chances to demonstrate their effectiveness.

A singer practices vocal control with singing lessons, a pilot logs flight hours at a flight school, accountants take accounting courses- your gift has a school of preparation too. Some schooling is formal, but not all education involves a building, instructors, curriculum and graduations.

When you can't afford training, teach yourself. Watch those that are doing what you want to do. Study them and dissect their achievements. Apply lessons learned to your own ambitions. If you're any good, you will notice small successes you can build on and put yourself into position to possibly gain entry into the training ground you desire with more competition.

Until then, find challenges and go practice your talents with and against others better than you. Find mentors and people willing to exchange insight. Though you may have an ideal arena in mind that would appear best to exercise your gift, do not exclude alternative paths. Especially since the more opportunities you take advantage of to develop and demonstrate your talent, the more expansive your frame of reference and experience is.

Despite how basic practice makes perfect seems, do not underestimate the benefits of repetition. Instincts are good to have, but natural talent only emerges into reliable expertise with good old-fashioned, persistent hard work. Test yourself by looking for real-world opportunities to validate your instincts and build confidence. Even an average person can show outstanding diligence.

Manipulation (is not evil)

Now that you understand the model of power and what your gifts are, using your power strands to get what you want is the mission. While some are waiting for chances given, others are taking chances living. It's up to you to decide which category you want to be a part of.

However, if you are ashamed of obtaining what you want in life because you fear the responsibility of success then much of what you are about to read from this point forward will be abrasive to your thought process. Also, if you are one that still holds dearly to the false notion that your life is predetermined and is out of your control, why did you pick up this book?

I believe you want to take action. You want to make it happen. Whatever "it" is for you, you are tired of waiting for it to be so.

You now need to set the stage for yourself. So manipulate for your own sake now. Please don't fear the concept of manipulation. Unfortunately the word "manipulation" has been judged unfairly as it is often associated with deception. But if perceived objectively, manipulation is only a means to control advantages by artful or indirect means.

The term "artful" suggests creativity. Indirect means are methods similar to playing chess: using pawns as decoys and knights to attack. Artful maneuvering means that you execute "the set up" to then make your move. While I do not advocate cheating, lying or hurting others, engaging your ambitions will undoubtedly mean encountering competition and opposition. This book is not meant to coddle or "sweet talk" you. So I'll make this clear: to manipulate is to manage and preserve your interest for your own personal greater good. You have a right to be happy and successful, just as you have a right to know how to achieve, protect, maintain and advance your power strands. We all manipulate to position ourselves for good outcomes.

Positioning yourself to make moves means setting yourself up to gain leverage so that your moves will have the power to succeed.

Anticipation and reliable instincts are needed. How well do you position yourself to achieve your desired outcomes?

First, know your surroundings well in order to recognize your allies, competition and enemies. Understand the parameters of your ambitions. Much like a stock broker researches market trends and public companies, you must investigate the realm of your ambitions to know and understand what will be demanded from you.

Educate yourself on all that relates to your agenda. Ignorance hinders both instincts and foresight. If you don't know what signs to look for, your competition will dispose of you easily as your naivety and inexperience will show.

Nobody reaches success without help from others. You cannot do everything alone. Eventually you will need support, favors, strategic allies, coaching, advice and maybe even someone to watch your back as you gain more power.

Sharpen your listening and observational skills. Setting yourself up to win involves reading situations and people then demonstrating an excellent sense of timing to know when to stay put or move forward. Learn to read people well and you can then maneuver, manipulate and even change situations.

Reading People
To the advantage of those of you that want power, the good thing about people is that we are not always dynamic. I believe individuals with the proper agenda, preparation, talent, ambition and drive can change the world in many ways. There is plenty of room for greatness.

People desire different things at different times. So while you may want to be promoted to supervisor or manager, your other co-workers may just want a paycheck. While you are plotting new and inventive real estate deals to own more property, most of the people you know are probably looking for cheaper apartment leases so they can start saving for a home. As you complete your master's degree, someone working an entry level job with only a high school diploma is happy to finally get health benefits after their 90-day probationary period. The term "average people" is not a myth, as millions of everyday people are just happy with life's bare essentials.

Some people don't want to be great, but just want to be. Some people don't want to change the world, but to only be a part of it. Some people don't want to be a part of change, unless it means more of the same. People don't frequently aspire to be different, but to just fit in and be normal.

I know you've heard people say things like: "They invented some kind of new thing. They discovered a new planet. They created some sort of new vaccine. They released some movie everyone's going to see."

Sarcastic as this reads, onlookers use the word "they" when referring to the mysterious cult of unseen forces that are locked away doing great things that only news reporters learn about. As if the top secret group known as "They" don't spend time living real life but only doing historical things to entertain everyday people. My suggestion to those that use the word "they" frequently: do not exclude yourself from greatness, ever.

Believe it or not, most people spend time listening, watching and reacting to the changes conjured by the mysterious group known as "They." If you find yourself always blaming changes or assigning advancements to "They," you need to be more proactive in your own life story. You need to start becoming a part of change so you can proudly claim "We" instead of "They."

Reading people means determining if people around you refer to changes as "They" or belong to the proactive party of "We." If you can decipher which people are followers and leaders attached to the circumstances surrounding your ambition, you will possess the driving forces behind your situations. Remember, circumstances are often people-driven.

When you are faced with individuals that are part of the circumstances surrounding your ambition, determine if the people you encounter are part of your problem or solution. Problems hinder your agenda. Solutions help your efforts. Both can be indirect or direct.

Followers are prospective support or distractions. Leaders are possible enemies or allies. In short, find out what makes people around you do what they do in the realm in which you operate.

Reading people first requires that you learn to be objective. If you are insecure, distracted by your own nonsense and hate being wrong, you can't read people well. Insecurity will cause you to be timid and cowardly. Unresolved personal issues can distract you from seeing truth or cause you to assign your own imbalanced characteristics to others. Pride will only cause you to see only what you want to be true. If you've got crap in your eyes, you can't see what's truly in front of you clearly.

See what's there, not what you want to see. Only you know how objective you can be, so internal honesty is mandatory. Lying to yourself or ignoring your own hang-ups ensures inaccuracy in your intuitive reasoning. Can you fairly access the motives and value of a fellow business partner when you're not confident in your own performance?

To read people, you must judge others. Beware, the idealistic side of you may scream, "No! I can't judge others!" But let's be rational- how else can you draw conclusions about others? You have to judge people to make decisive moves.

However, don't ever mistake judging for condemning. Judging others involves forming opinions based on the present reality in order to act decisively in your best interest. Condemning another means forming opinions on the present reality then adding your own imagined negative ending to ridicule or even punish another.

Don't prematurely imagine negative endings to other people's lives just because you may form a negative opinion of them in the present. Do judge others in order to decide if they fit into your forward path to power or not. When people don't fit into your agenda, wish the best for their path not the worst. If you wish evil on others, that's condemnation.

In addition, you do not determine the outcome of people's lives just because you judge them. People can always change. Perhaps you will not be around to see or experience the conversion. So don't ever assign finality to your judgments of others.

Unfortunately, the frequency of just how much we all judge each other is overlooked. The fact is that we must judge every day. When you make a left turn into oncoming traffic, you make judgments about the driver in the oncoming vehicle. He could be a maniac that wants to wreck his own car. He could be unaware of your turn. He could be a jerk that speeds up to cut off your turn. How would you know what sort of driver he is?

You pass judgment before you make the left turn. You put your life at risk every time you walk the street and assume the person walking past you won't suddenly pull out a gun or knife, go crazy and kill anyone nearby. We judge each other all the time, searching for honesty, establishing trust and boundaries just to interact among each other.

You've been reading and judging people your entire life. Now I'm challenging you to be even more aware of your intuitive process. In order to focus your instincts on the people creating the circumstances attached to your ambition, you must judge fairly and accurately to obtain the outcome you envision.

Recall your last job interview. You probably possessed all the necessary skills, just as the other applicants. So how does a recruiter hire only one person? A judgment is made by the recruiter about the personality type and skill sets needed for the position. Good hiring decisions are not based solely on resumes, skills or nice interview attire. Intuition is behind consistently good hiring decisions.

Hiring managers judge whether or not to hire you. Investors decipher if their money should go to your ideas. Banks judge your finances and sense of responsibility to determine if you get a loan or not. You are judged all the time, do the same by reading people.

What should you look for when reading others? That depends on your agenda. You'll never know everything about another person, so forget trying. However, you can attain their level of commitment, interest and compatibility with your agenda.

Determining friends or foes, is your focus when moving toward your goal. If you spot a foe, is the competition weaker, equal or stronger? If you find a friend, will the union be long or short term, strategic alliance or a genuine partnership?

Stay focused, whether in business or personal relationships. Objectivity means keeping your emotions in check and your impartial eyes open. "How does this person relate to my agenda?" That is the question you should ponder while meeting people somehow related to your ambition.

Sometimes people look for love, friendship and loyalty in places where competition and money is the priority not meaningful, sincere companionship. Other times people crave materialistic gains in matters and affairs of the heart. Know the difference or you'll find yourself wondering how to cope with the fact your so-called friend stole your idea or neglected to tell you all the terms and conditions of the joint investment that gives you a lesser split of the profits than you initially assumed true. Understand the difference between being loved and getting used by people that say they love you.

I despise watching people be naïve and passive about their dealings with others. It's nothing worse than seeing a good-natured person deal with someone exploiting them. Only to watch the decent human being say after the travesty, "What they did to me was wrong and they'll pay for it in the next life. They now have bad karma."

I'm not a big fan of depending on karma to watch my back or avenge my losses in this life or the next. Instead, I subscribe to the belief that we all have a right to be treated fairly now.

Do not ever forget this: you have a right to be respected. So begin all dealings with your best interest at heart. If you begin any relationship accepting unfair compromises gaining leverage and respect later will be extremely challenging for you.

As simplistic as that reads, I believe that we all have to remind ourselves every now and then. We sometimes forget we have a right to want what we want. There is nothing wrong with attempting to maintain fair dealings with others. It's only fair, right?

So many people find out just what friendships and marriages are made of when money is at stake or something of value must be divided or shared. That's when you see just how much you mean to someone. Supposedly no value can be placed on life and love, but that does not mean people will not try. Go to any divorce court and you'll see just how tangible the spoils of love can be.

When you are striving towards your ambition, don't hesitate to ask yourself the tough questions concerning the company you keep. Don't put off looking into the motivations of those closest to you claiming to be your support. Fearing harsh truths only increase the chances of encountering unexpected surprises later. Every now and then you should take careful inventory of the give-and-take balances in all your relationships. You have a right and responsibility to watch your own back.

If your strategic alliances, partnerships and personal relationships are in order, then your personal inventory of each will end well. If disappointing discoveries are made, you will have tough decisions to make. In any rise to power expect to witness and experience some casualties.

Imagine having to fire a family member who may be your favorite cousin but not up to the task of being your accountant. If you expect to obtain and maintain power over your ambition, be prepared to ask and answer difficult questions and resolve challenging obstacles.

Once you see the truth about a person and understand the current state of the situations related to your agenda, you are witnessing the foundation- it is what it is. Wishful thinking is fine, but even wishes are works in progress. Respect the reality of every situation first, see the foundation.

Spotting foundations means seeing things as they are in the present. Do not shy away from the truth as it is often just as simple as it looks. Before enacting your own building process, understand what you're building on first.

Recognize the Cycles

Reading people also means deciphering cycles of behavior. Did you know that sometimes, how people react to you has nothing to do with you? Sometimes circumstances affecting you did not begin with you. Many people allow the words; actions; and situations of others to influence them too much.

Ever had a friend that keeps making the same mistakes over and over again despite your good advice? How many people do you know that call you up and complain about every job they get? Have you ever worked with someone that always seems to get wrapped up in some sort of drama or brings their personal issues to business? Ever encountered a moody boss or routinely negative, pessimistic romantic partner?

If you have, there is a chance that none of what you encounter has anything to do with you! That's right. It's not your fault.

As a human being, you care about others. Nothing is wrong with caring as long as you know when to draw your own emotional line and realize the truth. What you are witnessing when you meet people or circumstances with reoccurring themes of difficulty is what I like to refer to as life cycles.

If you observe carefully, many people not only have routines in work and lifestyle, but personality mindsets as well. I'm pointing out that people you meet have life cycles, stages of behavior that change in a very specific order depending on the situation, time of year or even day of the month. Believe it or not, most people have consistent, conditioned responses to events in their lives.

Picture a co-worker that withdraws and becomes paranoid every time a new employee is hired because they fear for their job. Or a teammate that routinely challenges all authority figures. I once witnessed a young lady that would date men for six months, get dumped, be alone and depressed for three months, begin socializing for a month, meet a new man, date him for six months, get dumped, and so on.

Some people are literally creatures of habit. If you meet them at certain times of the year or during specific circumstances you will encounter their conditioned responses to whatever is going on in their lives. Almost like clockwork, human behavior can sometimes be measured as well.

If you are not aware when you have intruded on another person's personality cycle, you may assume you are involved in some way. You may even try and help only to meet frustrating, repeated failures that seem self-defeating to you as you try and figure out why someone keeps exhibiting the same responses to situations. Like stumbling and falling on a train track just when the train approaches, you can get caught up in someone else's life cycles.

The funny thing about the personality cycles of others you may encounter is that you become an interchangeable object to them. You're never unique to those trapped in a personality cycle. Anyone can be caught in the path. Ever seen that person that always has a sob story to share with anyone who will listen?

So I always tell myself: It is what it is. Do the same with people you meet. See them for who they are at the time you meet them not who you think they could potentially be. Look for behavioral signs that could be clues or predictors of how they respond to certain situations.

Yet never forget that people can change. But do not feel you need to be the catalyst for change in every person's life. Sometimes it is not your battle to wage or you may not even be equipped to deal with that person's situation.

The key to reading people and involving them in your plans is: assess the chances of people changing from the time you begin your agenda until you accomplish your goal. If changes are likely, anticipate if the change will be detrimental to your goals or not.

For instance, "Fred" may back your new marketing idea in the brainstorming session. But what are the chances of Fred bailing on you when it's time to present the new business strategy to the board of directors? Yes, predicting behavior can be challenging but hardly impossible.

Reliable foresight is a character trait in most successful people. Though you will not be right all the time, if you're on the money when it counts you've done your job. Human behavior can be unreliable, but not unpredictable.

Does that mean never to deal with a person unless you are absolutely sure they can live up to their potential when the pressure is on? No. See them for who they are at the time and determine if that is enough for you.

If it is, then any extra potential that emerges during your rise to power will be a plus. However if you encounter someone that doesn't exactly qualify for the role you need them to play, compare their potential to their desire and work ethic. If their potential, desire, work ethic and willingness to learn overshadow their weaknesses, taking a chance on their potential could bring pleasant surprises.

Just be mindful of personality cycles that may emerge and anticipate the effects on your agenda and rise to power. If you read personality cycles well you'll read patterns of events accurately. Once you understand the dynamics of the big picture you can effectively find and use your power strands of influence on the smaller pieces of life's puzzle and vice versa.

The Art of Persuasion

Persuasion is the nicer word for manipulation. Getting people to do what you want them to do is a necessity if you are to ever wield power in any form. Learn to manipulate the energies of others to your advantage with intuition, timing and skillful persuasive techniques.

Unfortunately, manipulation is a word frequently linked to deceit. But in all fairness, manipulation is neither a good or evil concept. The motives of people are what add negative or positive connotations to the word manipulation. Whether you manipulate for good or evil is up to you. But make no mistake about this: You will manipulate someone at some point in time to get what you need or want.

Look at the world around you. The difference between receiving a yes and a no from people is how and when you ask for what you need or want. If you ask the wrong way, you'll get negative responses. If you ask the right way, you may still not get what you want but very possibly polite rejections. But if you ask others for what you need or want in the right way at the right time, they become the right people to give you the support you desire.

The difference between mediocrity and greatness is your respect for time. Manipulation is best served when the time is best. Even if your presentation is not the greatest, timing can overshadow technique and grant you favor anyway. So you may stutter through your sales pitch in front of a group of buyers, but if the buyers planned on buying whether your sales presentation was Oscar-worthy or not, timing was in your favor.

That does not mean spare effort on learning how to communicate and persuade, but do master the art of perfect timing. Meaning, develop the instinct to sense when your time to influence emerges. We all have our moments of feeling invincible, unstoppable or supremely confident.

The perfect speech, the flawless game, the impeccable performance or the idea that came along at just the right time, all represent perfect timing. When the moment is right for you to advance you will see incredible amounts of power strands at your disposal. When operating your gift at the right time your execution will be instinctive, seemingly effortless. You will not only have what it takes to win. You will have no other choice but to act.

Even when obstacles emerge during your time, you will not waver. Your gift will manage you. Your talent and skill will sustain you. Time will welcome your success.

To elaborate, perfect timing is when preparation and opportunity join nerve, talent and execution simultaneously. Persuasion is only persuasion when desired results are achieved. Anything less is nothing but an uninvited interruption.

How can you demonstrate perfect timing? When you have prepared yourself; when the opportunity welcomes your sort of expertise; when you stand in the face of possible failure but still keep your nerve; when your faith in your talent is unwavering and you feel confident you will execute your best effort.

Persuasion is manipulation under the right cover of circumstances. Your words and efforts have more influence when change is possible and your audience sees opportunity in your agenda. Opportune moments are the results of your path meeting other paths that are in transition due to a need that must be filled.

Since change is inevitable, start to train your intuitive eyes to pick up on the signs of favorable circumstances related to your ambition. Like a meteorologist uses technology to anticipate weather changes, use your instincts to read and interpret the moods and behaviors of people related to your ambition.

How do they react to your presence? How do they respond to your words and ideas? How do they react to your successes and failures? What ways do they exhibit support for you? What are their limitations? How loyal are they? Are they friend or foe, strategic ally or long-term partner? All those answers matter greatly as you begin to exert perfect timing and execute tactical maneuvers to gain power.

Another aspect of persuasion that proves effective is what I like to refer to as "seed dropping" or indirect suggestive persuasion. Once you are comfortable recognizing opportunities that happen to cross your path, eventually you'll want to start being even more proactive in actually creating the climate of opportunity. Seed dropping is like subliminal advertising- a hint goes a long way.

Suggestive persuasion entails making indirect propositions not direct sales pitches or demands. As opposed to urging a person in one direction or the other, suggestive persuasion is founded on the inherent ability of people to make logical choices freely when presented information. When people have to make choices, we all assume that they will make the right choice. Yet what is right for one person may not be right to another. So to position your agenda as the right choice, you must appear to be objective in the eyes of those you mean to persuade.

The image of an unbiased communicator positions you in the minds of others as a trustworthy source of information. The perception of objectivity is established when you know your competition as if you are a part of their agenda. When you can intelligently present your competition's agenda as if it were your own while at the same time voicing your own agenda with equal skill, you empower listeners. All people want respect. You show them respect by presenting to them the opportunity to choose for themselves.

You'll be seen as confident and trustworthy, not just another salesperson. Inevitably, listeners will see you as an authority figure not a pitch artist. Eventually they will be interested in where your loyalties rest. When they see that you have sided with your own agenda because it is the logical choice, you may persuade others to do the same.

Positioning
With perfect timing you can even set yourself up for success. Establish your position. Then leverage your influence at the right time for desired results.

How?

Fill smaller voids somehow related to your agenda. Similar to buying up small lots of land and overlooked property in a bad neighborhood that is about to be targeted by real estate developers, positioning is about collecting small pieces to eventually use as bargaining tools in order to acquire a collective whole.

When the time comes, you will have invested enough time and effort to position yourself to get more than you originally sacrificed. When those developers need more land for their new projects, they will have to buy what you have in your possession. That means you have positioned yourself to leverage the influence you acquired gradually to cut yourself a pretty good deal and profit.

Granting favors, giving compliments, acknowledgements, completing grunt assignments and good old fashioned hard work can help put you into the position of influence. Volunteering, mentoring and some overtime hours go into your intangible investment portfolio. Sometimes you need more than desire, skill and ambition to gain favor. Accumulating favor by way of a series of persuasive investments improves positioning.

You may need to put in some time that gets your best results noticed by the right people. Networking or attending that cocktail party to schmooze may seem like you're puckering up to kiss where the sun doesn't shine. But legitimate talent deserves to get recognized and occasionally needs unique alternative stages to get noticed.

When the direct approach is not the best option, positioning comes in handy. Trying to close the deal or demand too much, too soon can ruin all of your previous accomplishments. Again, perfect timing means to recognize when it's your turn to capitalize.

Positioning is like a boxer's jab landing early and often to set up the big punch in later rounds. Or taking the entry level position not related to your college major just to get your foot in the door of an organization to have access to more lucrative opportunities. Like a majority stock owner or a star player that is close to the owner of the team, positioning is about building on small, sometimes intangible things to get leverage later when more tangible rewards are at stake.

At times you will be faced with the choice of being completely honest versus keeping your true agenda unknown. Though you may sit in a room full of co-workers claiming to all be a part of the same team, don't think that competition is not lurking. If your goal is worth your effort, value can be seen by others as well.

You may be a true team player that shares your ideas willingly offering everyone chances to share in your vision and process to be the best. Yet not everyone is so idealistic. There could be someone present that would like nothing more that to have exactly the same thing that you want. Never overlook competitive possibilities.

In some cases, you may need to keep your goals secret. Perhaps the tactic of surprise will give you an advantage later. When the time arrives for you to play possum and put on your best poker face. Convince your competition to underestimate you so that you can gain a surprising advantage later when you unveil your true agenda and ability. If you actually surprise your competition then they underestimated you, you better be able to pull it off. Laying low can backfire if you don't time your surprise perfectly.

Sometimes it is best to not broadcast your successes or agenda until you are certain you are among true friends and support. Meaning, you must gain leverage before you expose yourself. Your ideas may be great enough to steal or sabotage. Plus, stepping on the wrong toes without anyone watching your back could cost you. Don't allow a hidden speed bump or pot hole to suddenly appear in the road just because you couldn't keep your eyes open, mouth shut and your hand hidden from roaming envious green eyes of jealousy.

Another element about positioning is learning to pick your battles and win your wars. If you spend time waging every battle for every item on your agenda, pettiness will consume you. Understand that some battles are not worth ruining the opportunity to embark on more important ventures. Whining or pouting about every battle lost will distract you from the bigger picture.

A lost battle or even one surrendered does not mean your goal is unattainable. Avoid fixating on expendable agenda items by first prioritizing your needs from your wants. Fight for the needs, aim for your wants but plan on using expendable items as sacrifices for leverage needed to win most of your needs. That's what positioning is all about.

Trappings of Power...
With every notch of success you will start to witness the true feelings of those around you. Some will want to sincerely help your cause. Some will pretend to assist you for their own selfish reasons.

Some will defy you at every turn because you hinder their agenda or they simply despise your success. Others will go back and forth between supporting you and supporting others. So prepare to observe and experience many fluctuations in your environment.

This may seem harsh, but you better get used to this reality: you cannot make everyone happy.

Just because you get what you want does not mean that on your way to your goal you won't leave behind a few disgruntled people that feel used, neglected, cheated, overlooked, forgotten or even exploited. Despite your success being a thrill to you, don't be so naïve to expect everyone to be happy for you. This world is not always fair because people are not.

Sure you'll have genuine support and appreciation from those that truly are happy for you. Just don't be shocked when old co-workers, former business partners or even best friends subtly hint that you're "lucky" or "caught a break" you didn't really deserve or qualify for. When you are at your worst, people remember your worst words and actions. But when you are at your best, people have a hard time letting go of the past, especially if your past is not so perfect.

You may be startled to learn that associates and friends you struggled to get to the top with were really only close to you because your failures validated their letdowns. Unfortunately, some of your closest friends and family patronize your ambitions with fake smiles and hollow well-wishes. That is, until your dreams become reality and they are still living the way you used to live. That is when you'll see the difference between true support and hidden envy. Misery loves company and hates success even more.

You'll even encounter people that genuinely supported your rise, helped you gain influence then despise you for winning favor. Those types of people are really cynics with nice faces that don't believe the best can happen but are curious enough to pretend to support dreams just to try and capitalize off you. In their hearts they can't visualize happy endings and enjoy watching their predictions of failure come true but will gladly eat off someone else's full plate if given the chance. But when you prove their hidden doubts wrong they will turn on you or pretend to be happy and supportive until they can sabotage or betray you. If you aren't aware of their hidden natures initially, their betrayals will shock you to the core and hurt you deeply. Hence, choose your alliances and company wisely.

Especially since success often brings stiffer competition. Delusional minds assume that success is like arriving on easy street and vacation resort living all day, every day. To keep power, you must constantly exert and obtain even more power.

You want that raise at work then you must also want more responsibility. You want more real estate property then expect more demands from tenants. You want people to join your group, buy your product or invest in your idea- be prepared to deliver results consistently. More power equals more work.

Power is not for the weak, lazy or unsure. In the wrong hands, power fades, abuses or gets conquered easily. So if you obtain and maintain power be equipped to deal with it.

You will be watched, critiqued, criticized and challenged often when you get to the top. Others who do not know anything about you or what you sacrificed to reach your goals may speak of you unfairly as if they know you personally. Consumers, critics, competitors and regulating officials will not always be your favorite people. With power, you will not only have great responsibilities but be subject to the opinions, judgments and even condemnations of others. To make matters more difficult, sometimes it will not be in your best interest to offer your true feelings about what others think of you since some of your worst critics will be your customers or subordinates.

Think of that movie star that can't get into public altercations without getting sued or chased by paparazzi. Or the politician that can't openly state personal views on religion or sexuality without losing votes- power can be like prison at times. You will be handed unrealistic expectations and standards to live by as your consumers, critics, subordinates or followers look to you for things they could do on their own with more drive and ambition.

Yet you will be responsible for the actions of those affiliated with you, be blamed for failures not entirely your fault and your past may even be brought up to discredit or humiliate you if possible. Power draws plenty of smiles and handshakes but just as many or more rumors, gossip and back stabbing. Even more disturbing is that when you get power you may suddenly meet new family members you haven't heard from or even met before. Acquaintances that rarely spent time with you suddenly will call themselves your friends.

If not prepared for influence, people will be overwhelmed by newfound power. A poor person that suddenly becomes rich but is ignorant of how to invest and expand wealth may blow a fortune. A ridiculed person with low self-esteem that obtains power may abuse others. A naïve person with power could get exploited by liars.

Power can even diffuse your motivation. Lazy people that get power may relax even more. Extremely motivated people may suddenly get too content with success. Sometimes when on the cusp of obtaining a tiny glimpse of success, moderately successful people relax and become satisfied with partial advancements.

Sadly, some people are so used to receiving the bare minimum rewards for their efforts that even a small token of gratitude fulfills their thirst for power resulting in the depletion of their hunger for more success. Just because you get a compliment from your superiors or competition doesn't mean that you've finally made it. The deal is done when you see the raise on your paycheck, your name on the office door or receive that contract extension you were aiming for. Don't let a little success spoil your vision or hinder your positioning attempts. So power not only adds influence but exposes vulnerabilities as well.

Benefits of Power

On a more positive note, power can be an absolute blessing. With power comes privilege. You will have advantages that others simply do not have.

For all your hard work in gaining power, you will have access to more resources than others who have less power. You might even get breaks that others might not. Perhaps you will be able to provide a better life for your family and close friends.

Implementing change and having others follow your lead is possible. Power allows you to sometimes get the benefit of doubt before someone with less influence. Whatever power means for you, know that your credibility gets a boost when you have influence to legitimize your words and actions.

A chief executive officer gets larger bonuses, more vacation time and longer lunches while hourly wage workers are supervised by middle management. Real estate developers and property owners make huge profits by selling property while tenants pay rent. Ministers are often paid by the donations of church members. Movie stars get millions of dollars from consumers who pay to view a movie. Politicians may work hard as public servants but they also get perks from various associations. Power comes in so many forms and carries perks that not everyone will enjoy. More responsibility and risks should equal greater rewards as well.

Think about what kind of power you want. What are the benefits after you get your wishes? While the perks may not be your primary motivation, definitely reward your brilliance and smart work by enjoying your newfound influence. Be good to yourself when you reach your goal. Then create new agendas and aim for even more power.

Your self-esteem and confidence will feel like fire inside your heart as you exert positive energy that others around you will notice. Expect attention and admirers. Aspiring talent will seek your advice. Competition will want to join your agenda. In your hands, you may even get to mold someone else's vision.

Those dear to you will be proud of your achievements. Those that doubted you before will witness you defy their skepticism. Many who never knew you before will suddenly want to find out about you. With power, the opportunity to influence and even help others increases.

Upon reaching each level of success, information and opportunities previously unknown to you due to your former status may be at your disposal. Knowledge formerly beyond your grasp will present new ventures for you to explore while those without your power may not have access or the same opportunities. In the eyes of those not holding the amount of influence as you, your success is a reminder that change is inevitable and power is always accessible.

Yet there is still one last Superior Truth. The Third Superior Truth compliments yet supersedes the first two. Without fail, the Third Superior Truth not only makes change inevitable and power available to you, it adds a broader dimension to your idea of power.

Chapter 4: Higher Power Exists

The Higher Power Mindset
Everything you've read to this point is unified in this chapter.
You can survive, yet not live. You can be satisfied, but not fulfilled. You can fit in but never really belong. You can even like but never truly love. What you cannot compromise is your own vulnerability to the forward progression of time. So why settle for anything less than your own measure of truth and fulfillment during every moment?

Excuses and nurturing condolences have little effect on the nagging urge inside you now reminding you that your best time was squandered, has passed or yet to emerge. Be honest with yourself, don't you want to know how it feels to be truly fulfilled and excellent at something? Think of people you admire or are in awe of. Recall people that you have met or seen living gifted existences which inspire you to proclaim, "Unbelievable, amazing, outstanding! If only I would or could…"

You can. Power in your hands can get you the fulfillment and exceptional existence you seek. Unfortunately, I've found that the term "power" frightens many people. In fact, I believe that power has been unfairly maligned by society for centuries.

Early on while developing the content of this book, I entered my local library to reserve a discussion room for a manuscript review with a local book club. Out of curiosity, the librarian asked me the title of my book. I responded, "The Average Person's Guide to Power."

A skeptical frown appeared on her face as she apprehensively replied, "That sounds scary. You're not out here slinging ugliness to the people are you? You don't strike me as the conquer-the-world-by-any-means-type." Somewhat puzzled by her response, I reassured the librarian that I was not out to enslave the masses under my very own dictatorship. I simply stated, "This book is for people that want to find their own personal power to achieve things in life which fulfill their emotional, physical and even financial well beings along with their own definitions of greatness." The relieved librarian smiled and politely said, "Good. I guess you're ok. The last thing we need is more advice on how to abuse power!"

Hierarchies, corruption, violence, exploitation, manipulation, degradation, destruction and abusive control frequently are associated with power. Commonly believed is that the attainment of power inevitably results in the extraction of power from those ruled or influenced. Wars, greed and lies are pitfalls of influence. Power breeds jealousy, mistrust and lies.

I'm certain you can think of a controlling supervisor, corrupt politician or abusive authority figure you've crossed paths with. Such ugliness exists. Enough historical evidence of human errors, corruption and abuses exist to give us all apprehension about the nature of all forms of power. If we all decided to exclusively embrace only the deplorable essences of power, a hopeless, divided and depressing society of life would result. How would you feel residing in a world in which you only felt safe enough to love, respect and trust you? What would such loneliness feel like?

On the other hand, power should be recognized as a multidimensional force. Good things come from power as well. Public opinion can influence or even topple corrupt hierarchies, so freedom to express ourselves and make proactive choices is powerful. Genuine love, charity, acknowledgement and praise are effective aspects of influence. Most of all, at any point in time you can decide how you feel, see, react and enact while existing in this life. How powerful is it to know that you can literally do anything right now? That's right, anything. Though such power does not mean you should just do anything without considering the consequences, the point is you can actually do whatever you wish. Such access to choice is powerful. Your personal power and greatness is what this book is about.

There is no harm or shame in admiring greatness or wanting to be more than you are now. No honor exists in self-righteous humility adopted to hide the fact that you may have prematurely bought into accepting your failures by pretending your dreams were only bouts of immaturity or superficiality. Fake contentment usually produces regret and even jealousy toward those that prove to believe in and embody the power of excellence despite their imperfections. Maybe you've convinced yourself that you are now mature because you are so "realistic" or "grounded." Perhaps you've clipped your own wings to save the world the trouble of telling you that you can't soar. Have you given up?

Consider that there is still time for you to know what it feels like to be better than average. Aspirations of greatness do not always have to be dismissed as delusions of grandeur. Excellence is not a sin. Just as mediocrity does not equal righteousness. Common definitions of "real life" somehow excluded the possibilities of unexplained proof of seemingly miraculous exceptions. The only harm in greatness is not ever admitting that you want to be an exception to the status quo. Dare to be great.

Sure, crap happens. I'm certain you've endured personal breakdowns. Setbacks have occurred in your life and you want to know why so that you can begin to overcome cyclical failures with newfound truth and power. Hearing that "some things will forever remain a mystery," "that's just the way things are," or "everything happens for a reason" doesn't make losing your house to a natural disaster or back property taxes any easier does it?

You probably long for more money. Yes, you may be a modest person. But does humility have to go hand-in-hand with surviving check-to-check?

More financial security could be what you seek. Watching lifestyles of the rich and famous on television just doesn't give you that same thrill like it used to. You start to feel so jealous that you want to go tell that whiny celebrity complaining about not having any privacy, "Shut up, you make fifty million a year, go buy an island or something! If you didn't want people following you around with cameras then go marry a loser, have three kids, gain fifty pounds in the wrong places and take a job you're underpaid and underappreciated for!"

Increased respect in life could be what you seek. Sure you are a nice person, perhaps even too nice sometimes. But does politeness mean stifling or depreciating your own worth to protect the egos of others?

A lost purpose inspires your need for change. Maybe you forgot what you really wanted in life. Motivation can even go away or change once life takes on new or different meanings with age and experiences. Unfortunately, with time our ambitions can get sidetracked, altered or even lost completely. What excited you at 21 may not energize you at 30, 40 or 50 years old.

If you are part of a younger generation, getting started on the right path may be your goal. A sign that youth appreciates experienced advice is a blessing. I encourage all ages to read on.

Admit it. You want things your way now. An average life excites you about as much as an enema! So what's stopping you from making your life less average?

For the average person, it's the larger truth, the bigger picture-our world can be intimidating. Things can go wrong and plenty of obstacles exist. No one enjoys rejection or failure. Taking risks then failing at this point in your life could hurt you and even your loved ones. Your income does not compare to your ambitions or dreams and no investors are lining up at your door. Perhaps you come from an impoverished background without much encouragement. Maybe you don't have many friends or a reliable family structure. Or, you've failed so many times and are afraid to fail again but even more fearful of the responsibilities of success.

We all have fears. No doubt, life can be tough and seemingly unpredictable. In this world bad things happen to good people. Money seems to run from those that want and need it most. Love can elude people with the most love to give.

Unexplained setbacks haunt the paths of those already cornered by unfortunate circumstances. Just when things seem to get better, the worst takes place. Rich people claim money is the root of all evil and can't buy love. Yet people without much money say that money isn't the root of evil, people are evil- screw love!

Happiness has as many definitions as religious, scientific and political talking heads have followers. Love is defined by the endless ways people perceive what they can and cannot live with. Peace now equals harmony based on people agreeing to disagree. Truth is not determined entirely on facts but where the facts come from and why those specific facts were made known. Honesty often means information shared based on how much truth the receiver can handle hearing or how much information the messenger has to protect and hide. Morality now means "right for me, wrong for you."

In short, living among other human beings involves endless uncertainties, possibilities and differences among us. Taking risks, making changes as opposed to establishing reliable, consistent ways of living seems illogical. There is enough unpredictability in the world. The average person does not need anymore complications, right?

However, as dynamic as the endless life forces are surrounding us, there is hope for so-called average people. We have more influence than we think or embrace. Contrary to common belief, the average person possesses the dominance to predict and even create desired outcomes.

You don't have to put up with anything you don't want in your life anymore. Mark the upcoming words. After reading this offering you will no longer fear or feel uncomfortable about looking at circumstances or obstacles in defiance to say, "Things are going my way from this point forward."

Exceptional, extraordinary, superior, uncommon or special: all words based on the concept of greatness. If those terms do not describe you in some way, keep reading. The average person's guide to power is: The Higher Power Mindset.

Do you have it?

I'm no doctor or psychologist. I'm no preacher. I'm no movie star or financial expert. I'm not secretly some kind of genius with an intelligence quotient out of this world. Nor was I born rich or have parents that achieved unbelievable financial success- no trust fund pads my future.

I was an average person. I've accepted mediocrity before. Admittedly, there were times in my life when just the bare minimum to get by was a blessing to me. I've failed at many, many things.

I've been evicted from apartments four times. I've been fired and laid off more times than I care to remember. I've been homeless before while pursuing my dreams. I know how it feels to interview for jobs and not get hired even though I'm qualified. I know how it feels to dream big and fail hugely. I used to be so good at being "broke" I could make five dollars last me two weeks before I got hungry.

I graduated from college but also know how it feels to cash an unemployment check at a currency exchange because I couldn't get a bank account due to bad credit. I've had people try to destroy my life, ambitions and even personal being for no reason at times. I've been treated unfairly before, cheated out of opportunities and even betrayed by people I once trusted. I've reaped what I've sowed hundreds of times over. Frankly, my life hasn't always been one that I enjoy. If your hands cradle this book, there's a strong chance you've had your own personal challenges as well.

With the Higher Power Mindset I found ways to gain leverage and influence. I discovered ways to endure. There comes a time in your life when circumstances cannot matter and you simply must not just fight, but win.

Unfortunately, we often only hear life lessons from people deemed as enormously powerful public personalities or human saints. But where is the voice of the "average person"? If reality television and daytime talk shows are the answers, we're all in dire need of better representation.

Got money problems? Got a boss that works your last nerves, won't promote you or give you that raise you truly deserve? Is your business venture unadventurous? Is your love life missing an actual love of your life? Are you still planning your success instead of living it? Tired of coming in second or even last?

You may be trapped in the doldrums of the daily grind.

Every day the steps you take in the same old paths will confirm what everyone on that path knows to be true: you're no better or worse than they are. You're just like everyone else. The daily grind rubs out discrepancies and signs of unpredictability. Then "the everyday" shrinks your world into a reliable cradle of predictability. In this small world of complacency there is no need for hope and miracles, no hint of idealism survives. Everything is as it should be: normal.

Like a sign of integrity or even a right of passage, the daily grind tattoos its days, weeks and years on your face, walk and talk embedding the spirit of mediocrity into your being. Like a neutral pale brown color or neighborhood staple, you reside in this space of acceptance filled with lukewarm contentment. Some in this place of half smiles take great pride in not complaining, doing what needs to be done and not asking for too much to elude the unfortunate labels of: dreamer, ambitious, pretentious or fool. The crevices of the daily grind are filled with scattered broken dreams the way abandoned old buildings become eye sores in neglected neighborhoods. Many embrace mediocrity out of fear, disgust or self-imposed exile to hopefully forget those broken dreams, grow up and move on like good grown-ups should. The daily grind shows no mercy.

But prepare to learn something new about destiny and fate that the daily grind will not teach you. Luck is more than staggering coincidence. This book disproves that things are "meant to be the way they are" because "that's just the way the cookie crumbles."

Of course there are hundreds of books that claim to contain the answers that will improve your life. What works for people that prefer formulaic life improvement steps, daily planners, religion, exercise, meditation or sessions with mental health or life coaching experts, may not always work for all. Still, I commend and am grateful for all those attempting to help people live better, more purposeful lives. There is great honor in such aspiration.

Yet with so many purposeful messages to choose from, how does an average person pick the best one? Supposedly, no message is perfect for everyone. However, you are now reading the perfect book for you.

I caution you now that if you read any further you will be challenged to expand or even alter your point of view on perfection to begin to comprehend the remainder of this book. In this chapter, The First and Second Superior Truths come together. Of the Three Superior Truths that create the Higher Power Mindset, the Third Superior Truth is cohesively governs how you embrace, embody and behave with conviction under the Higher Power Mindset.

As you begin to take on the Higher Power Mindset, consider that perfection is not impossible.

Believe it or not, you witness and experience perfection every moment of every day. A rising sun, a rainy day, a newborn child and even death are all perfect. A healthy heart, cancerous lungs, 20/20 vision or blindness- all perfect. A new car driving the highway or a plane crash landing, still exemplify perfection. Before you conclude I'm a cold-hearted, insensitive sadist. Take into account the following.

The definition of perfection is misunderstood.

Sadly, most of the time we have difficulty acknowledging perfection because we are disappointed when reality does not conform to our idea or limited definition of what perfection should be. Our self-centeredness leaves us unaware of the presence of flawlessness all around us. In short, our point of view on the meaning of perfection is habitually biased.

Just as your idea or definition of "average" may differ when compared to another individual, your understanding of perfection hinges on what you deem as positive and negative in relation to your own beliefs, convictions and expectations. Because your surroundings may also encourage and validate your beliefs and perspectives, your vision can be molded and even enforced by others.

Your current understanding of perfection might be perfect for your surroundings and acceptable to others, but is it perfect for you?

This book now challenges you to discover your own perfection. To eventually see and accept the biggest picture that surrounds the bigger picture is to your advantage. You currently see what you want and have been told to see. Yet are you seeing all of what you need to see?

If not, you will. Understand the following about perfection: good or bad, negative or positive outcomes are all perfect. Your perceptions and preferences have absolutely nothing to do with perfection. If limited by how society has trained you to feel, view, understand and categorize outcomes, you then accept the consequences of losing broader insight.

No matter the socially labeled consequences, profound knowledge and truth rests in the actual processes of events and outcomes in life. Not just in how such outcomes are categorized based on human beliefs, convictions and wishes. To move beyond the confines of normal perceptivity into a heightened state of awareness, from this point forward embrace a new understanding of impeccability: exactness equals perfection. Truth is exact.

Begin to view your life and this world through truthful, exact lenses and experience increased depth and expanded vision. While others view immediate circumstances to make short sighted judgments and choices based on limited perceptions, you can see beyond with a Higher Power Mindset based on superior, broader truth.

Honest vision is central to The Higher Power Mindset. You will see more than the bigger picture. Your eyes will witness the very source from which the bigger picture originates. Your thoughts must build on acuteness to inspire truthful, effective logic and rationale. You will not become cold or insensitive. Instead you will experience a different, more intense flow of emotion and awareness than you do now. With the Higher Power Mindset you will embody more knowledge, wisdom and confidence in life due to the broader consciousness initiated by your elevated acuity. As a result, your emotional responses and behavior will begin to demonstrate the sort of calm purposefulness which produces desired outcomes.

Minus exact insight, you will mistake setbacks as reasons to quit and successes as excuses to become complacent. Emotions and cultural perceptions can hinder your ability to see clearly to make fruitful choices. Insecurities, fears, false beliefs and simple ignorance get exposed or unravel under circumstances that require exact insight.

This book will defy all your perceptual limitations to expose the exactness of our existences empowering you to reach your own personal best, your perfection- power.

How?

Perfection is possible only if it rests on the universal principles of exactness. Remember, exactness equals truth. You are holding the perfect book for you. Based on The Three Universal Superior Truths which are the foundation of The Higher Power Mindset, soon you'll discover that every aspect of your life relates directly to the Three Universal Superior Truths as well.

Embrace the content ahead and you will begin to feel and exert power as you adopt a new Higher Power Mindset. The type of mindset that can get you what you need and want no matter how average your life is right now. The Three Universal Superior Truths are the undisputable examples of perfection in thought that will translate into behavioral success.

However, skeptics will echo safer sentiments and claim that such a bold proclamation is unrealistic. On average, no message is perfect for everyone, right? Mediocre people live and die by what others deem as realistic and rely heavily on what the average rate of success is.

But anyone with The Higher Power Mindset knows at least one thing: on average, mediocrity never proved anything wrong. Change is inevitable. Power is always accessible. You've embraced the first two Superior Truths at this point.

Let's go a step further now: if you want to defy all hindrances prohibiting your agenda, from this point forward expand your idea of personal truth. To accomplish a mindset that lives always conscious of the first two superior eternal truths, embrace the third Superior Truth: Higher Power exists.

I'm not just referring to the obvious higher powers such as legal systems, government or military influences. Nor am I alluding solely to science, technology or business. All those powers are created, manipulated, exercised and enforced by mankind – results of human ingenuity and consciousness.

Instead, our focus now is on much more imperceptible power that adds unlimited significance to the Third Superior Truth. This power is an abstract influence, the subject and driving energy behind mankind's desire to understand existence. Truthfully, this power is the source of all existence and validates the first two Superior Truths.

What makes change inevitable and validates the First Superior Truth is our ignorance. We will never be able to create finality through human ingenuity because we keep making new discoveries in our world that require us to find new ways to understand and exist in our surroundings. The very air we breathe, water that sustains our life and solar system which encompasses us validates the core of the First Superior Truth, which could not exist without the Third Superior Truth.

The Second Superior Truth means that power is always accessible to you. The vastness of our life possibilities creates opportunities of human inventiveness to take hold. You can do anything. Consequences exist for every choice you make. Endless courses of action await your footsteps so choose wisely. This Second Superior Truth would not be possible if not for the First Superior Truth of change and the existence of Higher Power.

Though human language attempts to describe and even define the Higher Power, admittedly no one is completely successful at such a task. Much like trying to explain occurrences that baffle or overwhelm the senses, like miracles or near death experiences, putting an absolute omnipotent existence into the parameters of language and human perception is like trying to stare directly at the sun.

The best way to emphasize the Third Superior Truth and the existence of Higher Power is for us to consider nature, which is within our physical grasp and the foundation of our scientific explorations. If possible, go outdoors for a moment. Whether winter, spring, summer or fall I want you to step outside, take a deep breath, exhale and look up at the sky. As you read on, consider and appreciate our earthly environment. You experience nature every waking moment so such a frame of reference is easily accessible. Nature represents the very signature of the Higher Power.

Understand that the human race is always subject to the laws of Mother Nature, another example of the power hierarchy at work.

Think of the last flood, tornado, earthquake or hurricane that demolished our buildings and landscapes reminding us all of our vulnerability to natural elements. While we create planes to grace the sky, turbulence can easily send planes off course. As we plan shuttle missions into outer space, once there our technology is primitive compared to the vastness of our solar system. Even your favorite morning meteorologists deliver seven-day forecasts with hints of caution because weather conditions can change in less than 24 hours.

In all, we do not conquer nature. Through scientific ingenuity, we merely learn to adjust to what is imposed on us by understanding and ultimately respecting what affects us. No different from the feeding hierarchy among animals in the wild where survival of the fittest is the creed. At various times, we are reminded of the natural hierarchy of power when we get caught in one of nature's aggressive cycles of change. Without doubt, exhibited throughout our many natural laws and in every living organism on this planet there is something more powerful than our human ingenuity and beyond our full understanding.

Unfortunately, we still often find a false sense of security in our own means and even develop a sense of superiority over our natural elements. In science we seek to understand ourselves and this planet. In religion we aim to comprehend the source, purpose and consequences of life. Even ideas and beliefs about the meaning of death become topics of concern and discussion among us while others go so far to claim acute understandings of the afterlife.

We have made great strides in medicine, technology and space exploration. Hence, if we know what the weather will be on any given day we make travel plans in anticipation of our predictions being true. Often our anticipations are correct as air traffic, road travel and even space exploration are common happenings. Yet we are not always accurate.

Ever tried staring directly at the sun on a cloudless day? If you have, then you've endured a very humbling experience. Permanent eye damage and a massive headache may be your only accomplishment if you attempt staring down the sun too often. You will also be reminded of forces beyond your physical capabilities.

Religion is a source of mental and spiritual healing and hope for millions of people. Beliefs, morals, values and even convictions derive from religious followings that impact our dealings with each other. Traditions and rituals that signify respect, devotion and faith in that which is beyond human reason and revered as omnipotent comprise religious establishments. While different faiths and doctrines exist, all forms of religion center on the belief that something exists beyond human understanding that affects us in some way.

Science and religion have often conflicted. Since both science and religion deal with our very existence and the origin, meaning and purpose of existence on so many levels, naturally conflicts occur among those in each area of concern. The most common disagreement centers on how human life started. Many scientific minds believe in the evolutionary process, which is based on the idea that humans evolved into our present forms over the course of millions of years, just as animals evolved into their current physical types. In other words, the gorgeous model or movie star we pay $7 - $10 a ticket to see possibly evolved from monkeylike species we now pay to see at any local zoo. On the other hand, some religious doctrines have varied stories about how life on this planet came to be, some even conflict with scientific assertions. Human beings are thinking, feeling and quite opinionated species.

How does nature and religion relate to the Third Superior Truth that Higher Power exists? Mankind is prone to developing god-complexes and forgets that the Third Superior Truth is irrefutable no matter which perspective one embraces, religion or science. While theorizing and bickering over scientific details and religious beliefs, we take for granted a simply profound yet fundamental truth. We exist.

As obvious as our existence is, you need to understand just how significant your life is in relation to gaining power. Since you are a part of existence, you are also derived from the powerful source of all existence. It matters not whether you refer to the source of all existence as Brahman (Hindu), God (Judaism and Christianity), Allah (Islam) or embrace The Big Bang Theory from science- because the universe, our solar system, our planet and our lives are living proof of existence derived from a Higher Power.

Obviously numerous ideas about the source of existence fill our world. Mankind has always wanted to understand our own origins. How did our universe come to be? Why is mankind here? Both are questions pondered over as far back as each of our memories of history can recall.

We are an inquisitive, thinking species. Such ponderings are to be expected and encouraged. Religion credits supernatural influences for all creation. Science credits the processes of natural phenomena. To oversimplify the perspectives of both: science attempts to explain how, when and where while religion seeks to expose who and why.

Frankly, both science and religion are playing catch-up trying to make sense of much grander truths than any of our scientific natural laws and religious beliefs will ever encompass by way of our languages and forms of communication. But the one irrefutable fact that both science and religion agree on is quite simple: we exist. Please keep that fact in mind.

The evidence of our existence is where your Higher Power mindset should focus. It is a scientific fact that Higher Power exists. Just as religions positively express the existence of that which is referred to as God. Our existence proves there is Higher Power. Don't mistake the previous statement as a declaration that God is indeed as described by the pages of various religious books or doctrines. That is not my assertion.

What I mean is that Something exists that cultivated what we come to understand as existence. Something started all this life. Whether that Something used the Big Bang or Adam and Eve to populate the earth- something can take credit for the very air you now take into your lungs. Exactly what that Something is and how such a force operates among us remains open to debate. Regardless, we are here, alive and existing as we know to exist.

Though you may be reluctant to change your religious beliefs, adopt a new faith, alter your spiritual stance or even subscribe to the numerous religious doctrines available on this planet. If scientific minded, referring to the source of our existence as Allah, God or Brahman might not be your preference. At the very least as human beings we can all agree that Something is the architect of our existence. How you decide to refer to this Something is up to you. Personally, I decided long ago not to entertain the dispute between science and religion. To me it does not matter if life resulted as explained by a scientific theory or religious version of creation- I'm just happy to be alive and propose that we'll never really know exactly how we came to be.

With that in mind, logically you can embrace that beyond your own existence Something else does indeed thrive, as it did even before what we define as life. Humbling indeed and understandably intimidating once accepted, your physical life began and will end while existence continues onward. Not to diminish the uniqueness of your life, but all human beings much like other species on earth have a life span. Something established our life cycles. The Something that I refer to in the preceding paragraphs is the Higher Power that exists as the Third Superior Truth.

To go even a step further, I now challenge you to transcend manmade limitations and even your own personal beliefs into a mental and spiritual state that applies the three superior eternal truths to everything in your life- even your spiritual or religious beliefs. Change is inevitable. Power is always accessible. Higher Power exists. The Higher Power Mindset is based on all three Truths, which relate to every aspect of your life.

So nothing is off limits, dare to question everything you've ever been taught and even convinced of, challenge your own comfort zone. Sometimes candid self-examination is necessary for you to surpass your Inherited Self, beliefs, values and convictions then rebuild into a more powerful mindset conducive to change, power and a uniquely profound understanding of what Higher

Power means in relation to your passion. At that point, your true Higher Self can flourish beyond any limitations imposed on you by mankind in ways you once thought unimaginable.

Look around you. Every natural element has purpose. The sun centers and warms our solar system. Our oceans and lands support our societies. Animals live among us and in the wild fulfilling their roles. We breathe air.

Though all those natural phenomena are sometimes taken for granted, you should marvel at the distinctiveness of our universe. Nature is not aimless or coincidental. All natural processes are specific and characterized by outcomes. A tree is not accidentally a tree, just as we are not by chance human beings. Furthermore, nothing derives from nothingness. You originated from Something and have a purpose.

A multidimensional force of genius left us all to figure out the origin, function and purpose of existence. Admittedly, despite our most advanced ideas and beliefs in science and religion concerning the source of all existence, no human was present to witness the beginning of what we call time. There were no cameras or internet. No news crews covered the origins of existence. A how-to manual was not written and left for us to read.

Yet at this very moment we are alive trying to make sense of life. Science continues to ask questions that lead to more questions. Religion provides various beliefs concerning matters of faith. But I think we are all looking too far for the answers when what we seek is already available to us.

The Higher Power that I speak of is already inside you. At birth you have it. It is the very core of your passion and from the origins of existence. Your passion gives you purpose the way the natural process of rainfall nurtures our lands.

Feel your heartbeat. It pumps blood. If it is a healthy, natural heart it beats without a battery or pump. Like the sun burns hot enough to warm our solar system without exploding to destroy us, a healthy heart pumps blood through veins. What's astounding is that the sun does not just explode and a healthy heart does not just stop beating until death. Something keeps the sun in place and our hearts pumping blood yet we can't see the driving force.

Inside of you burns a passion for something. Your passion inspired you to pick up this book. You want to find ways to get power to release your passion. Faith in the existence of Higher Power is needed.

For the religious, such a statement is a confirmation. For nonreligious or spiritually stagnant persons, talk of Higher Power reminds of religious doctrine. I am not endorsing or condemning any particular religious or spiritual belief. I am advocating that science and religion are perfect examples of just how important mankind's need to understand our origins and purposes of existence.

Science may claim that a big explosion resulted in our existence, but what caused such an event? Religions may claim that a supernatural presence created us all, but how can such a presence be completely defined by that which it created? Understand that you can only control and know so much before a loss of control and lack of knowledge is experienced. At that point, you need faith in Higher Power. Where our feelings, sights, perceptions, knowledge and understandings end- Higher Power prevails on. Your passion is part of this Power I speak of. It will help sustain your faith.

Picture your passion much like the sun. It exists. Your passion exudes power. It has the power to explode and destroy or grow and nurture. But much like the sun, no one really knows how your passion came to be. Yet you feel it. Sure, your parents may attribute your passion and talents to your family tree. But one question still remains: how did your passion come into existence in the first place?

Your passion is what drives you. It challenges you to act. Passion does not rest. If it ever ceases it is because hopelessness prevailed. Yet passion can still reluctantly exist in the form of regret and nagging impulses to act. Passion's purpose differs from one person to the next but the core of passion is a burning desire to see something through from start to finish through good and bad times.

It is your passion that this book wants to help unleash into manifestation. But your passion did not just emerge from nothing. Your passion derives from Higher Power.

As a result, you are free and empowered to adopt personal spiritual beliefs that support your passion. If you truly adopt the concept behind the Third Superior Truth, knowing that Higher Power exists means you are not limited by mankind's interpretation of what Higher Power means. To limit the meaning of Higher Power is to limit your passion.

To ignore Higher Power is to fail to believe in change, limit your power and live with no purpose. What a disgraceful waste of time and life. Higher Power grants you the intangible skill of intuition and provides you with the priceless ability to gain favor and inspire others. Most of all, Higher Power is individualized.

Millions of people find comfort in their chosen faiths. Christianity, Islam, Hinduism, Buddhism, Judaism and other organized forms of religion fill our planet. All faiths center on the belief in Higher Power. Our belief that positive ethics are important in human relations leaves our social behaviors vulnerable to religious influence.

Religion helps many people make sense of the unexplained and add conviction to their moral obligations. It also provides believers with a common bond that creates a sense of unity and inclusion. Fellowship, prayers and charitable goodwill can emerge from the power of religion. Faith continues to instill hope in the lives of people that rely, sometimes exclusively, on their religion for guidance and personal growth. If religious traditions were not useful to so many, multiple variations of it would not exist.

Yet it is the extensive variation of religious faiths that can create extreme religious fundamentalism, competition, self-righteous fervor and even religious separatism. Believers dispute among each other and divide over matters of doctrine, biblical interpretations and issues of morality. Religion, much like politics, is not immune to conflicts that ultimately divide entire movements of faith into one group against another. Even religion contains internal divides over issues like abortion, capital punishment and gay rights.

I heard an intriguing tale once that went like this:

One day in the Land of The Blind a mysterious beast arrived. The three wise blind elder authorities approached the mysterious beast. The first blind elder walked up to the beast, touched it and said, "I declare. It is definitely a tree trunk."

The second blind elder walked up to the mysterious beast, touched it and shouted, "No. I declare. It is a spear."

Finally the third blind elder walked up to the beast, touched it and claimed, "Both of you are wrong! I declare. I have no doubt it is a snake."

As the three wise blind elders debated, the people of the Land of The Blind listened intently. All three wise blind elders passionately expressed their points of view. But no agreement was reached. As a result, the Land of The Blind divided into three new provinces.

The Trunk Lands was ruled by the first blind elder and inhabited by all the people that agreed the mysterious beast was a tree trunk.

The Spear Province was ruled by the second wise blind elder and inhabited by all the people that believed the mysterious beast was a spear.

The third province became Snake Country, ruled by the third wise blind elder and inhabited by people that believed the mysterious beast was a snake.

What was the mysterious beast all three wise blind elders touched?

The first elder touched a leg. The second elder touched a tusk. The third elder touched the trunk. All three elders touched one part of the mysterious beast: an elephant.

Do you think the three wise blind elders understood how to expand their own personal perceptions of truth? If the people following the three wise blind elders had decided to discover truth for themselves instead of listening to the three wise blind elders, would The Land of The Blind be divided? That tale should confirm three things to you.

One, never allow someone else to think for you. Two, no one owns the truth because we all have valuable pieces of reality to share with each other. Finally, the truly wise know one thing: there is always more to know.

Unfortunately, our current religious environment is much like the Land Of The Blind. Depending on your religious beliefs, I'm certain you have a name for the Higher Power you pray to and worship. Or maybe you're an atheist with no belief in the concept of a Deity or deities being involved or concerned with human affairs at all. Maybe you're agnostic or non-theistic, committed to the position that since we'll never know for sure if God exists and operates the way religious doctrine states, why bother making a judgment at all?

For many, belief in a Supreme Being or supernatural forces is the foundation of what separates humans from animals. If a Deity or deities exist that are partial to human life then human beings have a higher purpose and obligation to the gift of life. Beliefs, convictions, morals and behavioral ethics derive from the belief and faith in supernatural forces. Religious movements and powerful institutions rest on faith in the existence of deities. Wars have been fought in the name of God. Religion and politics have often been the center of numerous conflicts as the personal beliefs and faiths of individuals become relevant in the realm of social reform and governmental influence. In short, how you view what Higher Power determines how you decide to exercise your passion.

So remember the following as you examine your own personal spirituality. All religions have evolved and diversified in some way and must also face an inevitable conclusion: though belief in supernatural forces can inspire goodwill and hope among mankind, the supernatural cannot be fully described or defined by mankind's greatest, most sincere efforts due the inherent imperfections and limitations of human perception and language. Yet our religious environment frequently attempts to do so.

All religions based on love, truth and goodwill should leave endless room for spiritual interpretations considering the mysterious vastness that the source of existence represents. Much like the validity of scientific hypothesis and natural laws are always influenced or even negated by information from new discoveries. If spirituality ceases to be dynamic, imbalance and intolerance emerges. Religion is the result. Religious separatism soon follows. Doctrinal powers attempt to own, control and even profit from versions of supposedly sacred truths by claiming absolute righteousness over all other versions of religious thought. Ironically, sometimes religion limits the very Higher Power it attempts to embody.

What your new Higher Power Mindset should embrace now is that your passion responds best to the version of Higher Power that changes and inspires your agenda in a positive way. People meet the personal face of truth at different times in various ways. Do not let someone else's inspiration of truth be the end all be all for you when you must ultimately discover and embark on your own path. Nor should you condemn someone else for not believing the way you choose to believe.

We are all wrong to try and monopolize truth. It has been said that a house divided cannot stand- consider The Land of The Blind. Perhaps all religions based on truth, goodwill and love have one universal element in common: all positive beliefs represent a tiny clue to a much larger Supernatural Truth.

Recall how we discussed positive, negative and neutral energies in the second chapter. The more positive energy you channel and exude, the more you will embody the sincere truth derived from remaining spiritually dynamic. Vast amounts of unseen truths are at your fingertips when you have faith in more than what you can see, touch, smell, taste and hear.

Mindsets of every human being you encounter have been influenced directly or indirectly by the very intangible mystery that science does not recognize as supernatural and what religion attempts to characterize with doctrine, rituals and words.

Your undivided attention and understanding of this superior influence grants you awareness beyond your physical senses that can lead you into realms where spiritual influence manifests into physical existence. I do not speak of religion, superstitious beliefs, witchcraft, voodoo, psychic ability or magic. I am referring to the sort of power that gives your thoughts, impulses, intuition and even physical senses something extra beyond even your anticipated needs, talent and skill.

What is it you want to achieve? You should always envision your desired outcomes. More importantly, understand that your visions do not start off as mental images but feelings. It is those feelings that your mind adds mental images to for you to envision your goals. So ask yourself, what feelings add life to the core of your visions?

Much like Higher Power, you can't see feelings but you can experience them. Your actions are evidence of your feelings just as our natural existence is evidence of Higher Power. Those feelings at the center of your visions represent your direct connection to your Higher Power- your passion.

Even more amazing is that your passion is much like your body's DNA. No DNA is the same between humans so we are definitely unique. In a sense, your passion is a sort of spiritual DNA. It gives you an intangible identity unlike anyone else. Though people may at times have passions for similar things, how and why they exercise their talents differ.

So your Higher Power is your personal truth alone. The reality for us all is that when we die the only beliefs that will matter most are not those of science, religion, or our dearest loved ones, but our own. After you're deceased, you'll be a part of what science and religion can only speculate about. Hence, never limit your idea of Higher Power and your power and passion will be infinite.

Embracing that change is inevitable means you will never stop growing spiritually, intellectually, psychologically and emotionally as an individual. Adopting a power mindset to see that power is always accessible means you will consistently be proactive in creating, implementing and executing solutions to empower your agenda. But it is the third superior eternal truth that will provide you access to unlimited power to enhance not only your visions of success but ability to really maximize your potential while remaining humble during your successes. So claim your power now. If you're sick of being average be extraordinarily determined to defy mediocrity.

Consider time carefully. Mankind created the concept of seconds, minutes, hours, days, weeks, months and years to measure and attempt to manage time. From the sundial to the digital clock, the human species found precise ways to try and harness the very concept of time.

But as your digital clock displays numerical values to time right down to the millisecond, understand that time is not such a simple reality to grasp. Time has irreplaceable value. Not only because we have not figured out a way to stop, reverse time or physically transport ourselves into the future. Time's essence is even more profound than we give due.

Time is irreplaceable since it originates outside the parameters of our understanding of existence. Though we keep track of time with our clocks, human beings are similar to children walking into a surprise birthday party. Just as the kids enter, everyone screams, "Surprise!" The children realize that they just walked into a party that was already in progress.

Time can surprise us at any time since time's existence did not begin with our awareness and creation of ways to keep track of seconds and monitor the rising and setting of the sun. Time is a supernatural reality with an origin and destination beyond our scientific calculations. We're like kids walking into the surprise party celebrating our existence, but the party was already in progress. Before you know it, you're too late, too early, too old, too young or too inexperienced to take advantage of time. Use time wisely and time will use you.

Think back. Recall one decision that you regret to this day. Looking at the effects of your choice, ask yourself the following: If you had the Higher Power Mindset at that time, how different would your life be now?

Unlimited power awaits mindsets that understand how to transcend the limitations of mankind. With the Higher Power Mindset you will tap into the intangible influences of Higher Power while still embodying your own personal version of human genius. Then you can achieve greatness.